MW01038387

ELVIS

Publications International, Ltd.

Written by Susan Doll, Ph.D.
Contributing writer: Richard Buskin

IMAGE CREDITS:

AFP; AP Images; AP Wide World Photos; **AP Wide World Photos:**
Greg Campbell, Tina Fineberg, Troy Glasgow, Mark Humphrey,
Stephan Savoia; Bill E. Burk Collection; Maria Columbus Col-
lection; Susan Doll Collection; Sharon Fox Collection; **Sharon
Fox:** Sam Griffith, Dave Szarzak/White Eagle; Getty Images;
Globe Photos; **Globe Photos:** Bob East; Sam Griffith Photogra-
phy; Heavenlea Productions; Dwight K. Irwin; June Juanico;
Bob Klein; Joseph A. Krein; Karl Kummels; Courtesy Bernard
J. Lansky Collection, www.lanskybros.com; Paul Lichter's Elvis
Photo Archives/elvisunique.com; Loew's Inc.; Dave Marsh;
Roger Marshutz/Motion Picture & TV Archive; MGM; MGM/
United Artist Home Video; Million Dollar Museum; Movie
Market Ltd.; NASA; National Archives; NBC Photo; NBCU Photo
Bank; Michael Ochs Archives/Stringer; Paramount Pictures;
Personality Photos, Inc.: Howard Frank; Photofest; PIL Collec-
tion; Courtesy Playhouse on the Square Archives; Elvis Presley
Museum; **Retrofile:** PLP/Popperfoto, SAC/Popperfoto; Ger Rijff
Collection; Rockin' Robin Rosaaen~All The King's Things Col-
lection; Michael Rutherford; **Showtime Archives:** Colin Escott;
SuperStock; SuperStock: William Hamilton, Michael Rutherford;
Dave Szarzak/White Eagle Studios; Time Life Pictures; 20th
Century-Fox Film Corporation; United Artists; Steve Vidler; Andy
Warhol Foundation for the Visual Arts/ARS, New York; Brian
Warling Photography; Warner Bros. Inc.

Colorizing by Cheryl Winser.

ACKNOWLEDGMENTS

Passages, reprinted by permission, are excerpted from *Elvis Up
Close By Those Who Knew Him Best* by Rose Clayton and Dick
Heard; Turner Publishing, Atlanta, 1994. Quotation from *TV
GUIDE*® magazine courtesy of TV Guide Magazine Group, Inc.
"©1956 TV Guide Magazine Group, Inc." Excerpt from *Films in
Review,* by Henry Hart. Copyright © December 1965. Used with
permission from Roy Frumkes, editor *Films in Review.*

Special thanks to Bill Burk, *Elvis World Magazine* and Lea Fryd-
man, www.elvispresleynews.com.

ADDITIONAL COPYRIGHT INFORMATION

"Don't Be Cruel" sheet music cover © 1956 Shalimar Music
Corp. and Elvis Presley Music, Inc., music and words by Otis
Blackwell and Elvis Presley; *Love Me Tender* © 20th Century-
Fox Film Corporation; "Elvis, An American Trilogy," single ©
BMG/RCA Victor; "Heartbreak Hotel" single © BMG/RCA Victor;
"One Broken Heart for Sale," single © BMG/RCA Victor; Elv1s
30 #1 Hits, CD © BMG/RCA Victor; *Elvis Aloha from Hawaii via
Satellite,* album © BMG/RCA Victor; Elvis and His Show poster
© BMG/RCA Victor; *Elvis at Madison Square Garden*, poster ©
BMG/RCA Victor; *Elvis Is Back!* © BMG/RCA Victor; *Elvis Presley
album* © BMG/RCA Victor; *How Great Thou Art,* album © BMG/
RCA Victor; *Elvis on Tour*, documentary © MGM; *Jailhouse Rock*
© MGM; *Kissin' Cousins* © MGM; *G.I. Blues* © Paramount Pictures
Corporation; *King Creole* © Paramount Pictures Corporation;
Flaming Star © 1960 20th Century-Fox Film Corporation; *Wild
in the Country* © 1961 20th Century-Fox Film Corporation; *It
Happened at the World's Fair* © 1963 MGM; *Viva Las Vegas* © 1964
MGM; *Roustabout* © 1964 Paramount Pictures Corporation, Hal
Wallis Productions; "Baby Let's Play House" © Sun Records;
"Good Rockin' Tonight" © Sun Records; "Milkcow Blues Boogie"
© Sun Records; "Mystery Train" © Sun Records; "That's All
Right" © Sun Records; *Kid Galahad* © 1962 United Artists
Corporation; "Decide Which Elvis Is King" promo © U.S. Postal
Service; *Dead Elvis: A Chronicle of Cultural Obsession,* by Greil
Marcus; *Early Elvis: The Tupelo Years,* by Bill E. Burk; *Elvis and
Gladys,* by Elaine Dundy; *Elvis: His Life from A to Z,* by Fred L.
Worth and Steve D. Tamerius.

This publication is not licensed by or authorized by the Estate
of Elvis Presley or any of its successors.

Copyright © 2023 Publications International, Ltd. All rights
reserved. This book may not be reproduced or quoted in whole
or in part by any means whatsoever without written permission
from:

Louis Weber, CEO
Publications International, Ltd.
8140 Lehigh Avenue
Morton Grove, IL 60053

Permission is never granted for commercial
purposes.

ISBN: 978-1-63938-410-5

Manufactured in China.

8 7 6 5 4 3 2 1

CONTENTS

ELVIS PRESLEY?

In the time it takes to read *Elvis*, you will learn enough about him to understand his significance in popular music and history. The key notes are all here: the roots of his music, the public storm over his provocative style, his important songs and albums, the changes in his career, and the fan phenomenon.

In addition to these high points, the full story of Elvis Presley also involves the flops, the bad movies, the controversies, and the poor choices that plagued him. You'll learn how these factors affected his music and his career and how they colored popular and critical views of his work. Most importantly, you'll see how these successes and failures combined to propel Elvis into the role of a uniquely American icon—a mythic figure who looms large in the public's consciousness, fans and otherwise.

Of course, not every memorable song, quote, or detail could be included in this book. But there's enough here both to inspire the uninitiated to explore the King with more depth and to remind lifelong fans of their favorite songs, movies, and memories.

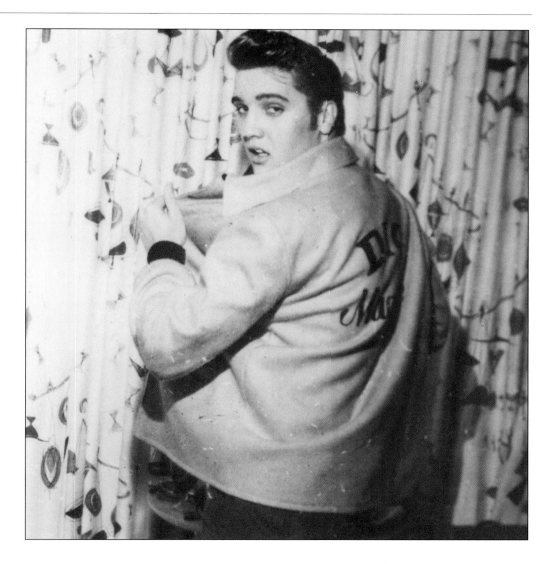

EARLY YEARS

Elvis Aron Presley was born to Vernon and Gladys Love Presley on January 8, 1935, in East Tupelo, Mississippi. Like many residents of East Tupelo, the Presleys were poor. They lived in the two-room shotgun shack (seen here) that Vernon had built the previous year. The little family moved several times when Elvis was a child, and Vernon worked at a number of jobs to support his wife and child. Despite many hardships, the Presleys were close to their extended family in the Tupelo area, and they enjoyed belonging to the First Assembly of God Church. In September 1948, they moved to Memphis because the city promised better job opportunities.

Elvis learned how to play the guitar in Tupelo and showed an early interest in music. In Memphis, he was exposed to gospel, rhythm-and-blues, and country music, which he would later integrate to form his unique sound. Music became the path that would lead Elvis and his family to a better life.

Elvis Presley "is a mystery that may never be solved."

—Journalist Nick Tosches

The close-knit nature of the Presley family is evident in this portrait of Vernon, Elvis, and Gladys in Tupelo.

GLADYS LOVE SMITH PRESLEY

Elvis Presley's Mother, Gladys Love Smith, was born in the flat farmland of Pontonoc County, Mississippi, not too far from Tupelo. Born into a large clan, Gladys shared what little the family had with seven brothers and sisters. Her father, who was a sharecropper and possibly a moonshiner, died when she was a teenager. She was forced to work to help support her family because her mother was sick with tuberculosis. When she was 21, she met handsome Vernon Presley, who was 17 years old. After a whirlwind

Gladys's life before she was married is seldom explored and therefore a bit of a mystery.

two-month courtship, the couple married, but they lied about their ages on the marriage license. She said she was 19, and he claimed to be 21. On January 8, 1935, Gladys gave birth to Elvis Aron and his stillborn twin, Jesse Garon.

In an Elvis Presley story in which myth is often mistaken for biography, Gladys is rendered as the hovering mother of the 20th century's most famous entertainer as though her identity consisted entirely of that relationship. She is described as the overprotective mother who was unable to leave her son in the care of anyone else for any length of time. She supposedly defended Elvis with a broom whenever boys picked on him, and it is said that she walked him to and from school until he was an adolescent.

Certain biographers have used the memories and stories of eyewitnesses to assert that this behavior toward her son was reasonable; others use those same stories to claim this behavior was odd or peculiar. Still others point out that the stories themselves have been exaggerated through retelling. Most photos of Gladys show her already in middle age. She is the melancholy, heavyset woman in a plain dress who stares out at the viewer with dark eyes made even darker by the circles beneath them.

But who was Gladys Love Smith Presley? What was she like as an individual in her own right? Did she have aspirations and dreams? Was she filled with satisfaction or regret?

As a young woman, Gladys was a tall, shapely, attractive lady with thick dark hair—a sharp contrast to her later photos. Though high-strung and nervous, she could also be bubbly and talkative. She had not been a good student in school, but she liked to interact with other boys and girls.

As she grew older, Gladys continued to enjoy being with people, and her dark, sultry looks attracted the attention of country boys with nicknames such as Pid and Rex. She also socialized at the Church of God and Prophecy in Union Grove.

Despite a life of privation in the backwoods of the Deep South, Gladys had access to the 20th century's two biggest contributions to mainstream culture—recorded music and the cinema. Her neighbors down the road, the Reeds, bought a Victrola when she was teenager. Some of the first records she heard were by Jimmie Rodgers, a country-western singer who was also from Mississippi. The young country girl danced a wicked Charleston to his music with such energy and jubilation that old friends and neighbors remembered it long after she was dead. She had an innate sense of rhythm and a passion for music that

Vernon, Elvis, and Gladys Presley say goodbye on March 24, 1958, the day Elvis was inducted into the Army. Gladys looks distraught as Elvis prepares to leave for Fort Chaffee, Arkansas.

inspired her to dance with bold abandon.

Gladys met handsome Vernon Presley after she moved to East Tupelo to work in a garment factory. She liked working in the factory, not because the work was interesting but because of her camaraderie with the other girls. During her early marriage, the vivacious young woman remained spunky, talkative, and eager to socialize, especially at the East Tupelo Assembly of God Church. Gladys, Vernon, and their friends and family loved to sing gospel music together, harmonizing on such standards as "The Old Rugged Cross."

As the years rolled by, economic and personal hardships took their toll, and the spunky young woman with a love of music

Dr. William Robert Hunt

Dr. William Robert Hunt delivered Elvis Aron Presley on January 8, 1935. He was 68 years old at the time, and the Presley twins were the 919th and 920th deliveries of his career.

Dr. Hunt, known as the "poor man's doctor," charged very low fees, even within a poor county in a Southern state during the Depression. He treated local mill workers, examined Army draftees and inductees, and took the welfare cases. His daughter, Sarah Hunt Potter, affectionately called him "an old country GP who poked along and never got ahead of himself."

Elvis was born in this modest house on Old Saltillo Road in East Tupelo. Elvis's grandfather, Jessie, raised it off the ground with field stones to prevent flooding.

But he was much more than that. The delivery of Gladys Presley's twins had been a difficult one, and he sent her and her remaining twin to the hospital after the births. He was responsible for restoring her health and preserving the health of her infant. That this baby grew up to change the course of popular music did indeed make Dr. Hunt a significant figure.

Unfortunately, the good doctor did not live to see this occur. Dr. Hunt died in 1952—two years before Elvis recorded his first singles for Sun Studio.

and a gift for dancing faded away. Gladys remained warmhearted, friendly, and gracious, but she grew into a nervous middle-aged woman, especially regarding Elvis' safety. Responsibility and concern over the well-being of her only son consumed her.

Gladys is generally painted as a tragic figure because her life was hard by contemporary standards, and she died at the relatively young age of 46 in August 1958. Few offer a fuller portrait of the fun-loving country girl who danced the Charleston with wild abandon. While the two extremes are difficult to reconcile, Gladys will always be remembered for her depth of love for her son.

VERNON ELVIS PRESLEY

Vernon Presley was as sober and dour as Gladys was warmhearted and outgoing. By the time he met pretty Gladys Smith, he had also experienced his share of hardships. He did not enjoy a close relationship with his father, the hard-drinking, hotheaded Jessie D. McClowell Presley, who kicked the unfortunate lad out of the house when he was only 15.

After Vernon and Gladys eloped on a whim, they had no place to live. Vernon dreaded telling his father, known as JD, about the marriage, because the elder Presley had never had a kind word to say about this particular son.

The tightly-knit family of Vernon, Gladys, and Elvis found their lives turned upside down when Vernon was sent to Parchman Prison, a penal plantation in the delta region of Mississippi where the inmates worked the land in chain gangs. In November

Gladys, Elvis, and Vernon make a somber group as they pose for a photo not too long before Vernon was sent to prison.

1937, Vernon was indicted for forgery, along with Gladys's brother Travis Smith and

Lether Gable, and sentenced to three years in prison. The sentence seems harsh considering the crime: Vernon, Smith, and Gable had altered the figures on a check to Vernon from Orville Bean. Bean owned the land that Vernon had built his house on and frequently hired the young man as a laborer. Vernon sold Bean a hog for four dollars but felt the animal was worth a lot more and altered the figures on the check to compensate.

The incident provides a snapshot moment of the Presleys' life in Tupelo. Elvis's poor childhood in the shotgun shack has become such a clichéd part of his life story that their abject poverty is lost beneath quaint stories of family togetherness and gospel singing at the Assembly of God Church. But this story is neither quaint nor colorful. Not only did Vernon's stint at Parchman result in the loss of their tiny home, but it also made it more difficult for him to find work.

After his release from prison, Vernon continued to work at a variety of jobs, moving his family from relative to relative, finding permanence in neither job nor home.

"Parchman Farm Blues"

About the same time that Vernon was incarcerated in Parchman, a bluesman named Booker T. Washington White may also have been a "guest" there. Nicknamed Bukka, White had been convicted of assault in 1937 but jumped bail and traveled to Chicago, where he recorded two songs. He was caught and returned to Parchman to serve a three-year sentence. After his release, he returned to Chicago to record 12 new songs, including his own composition, "Parchman Farm Blues."

KINFOLK

Elvis not only felt a deep bond for his mother, but he was also close to his aunts, uncles, and cousins. After he became successful, he took care of many of them financially, just as some of them had taken care of Gladys and him during those early years in Tupelo.

One of the most colorful Presleys was Vernon's brother, Vester. As their names might suggest, Vernon and Vester, who were the oldest of J. D. Presley's children, were very close while growing up. They did chores together, and they got into trouble together, including the time Vester lowered Vernon into the family's water well but was not strong enough to pull him back up again. If he had let go of the rope to get help, the bucket would have slipped all the way into the water, and Vernon would have drowned. Vester had to hang on to the rope until his parents returned.

Vester and Vernon were constantly playing practical jokes on each other, and the habit was carried over into their adult lives. Like Vernon, Vester worked any job he could find to feed his family, including selling whiskey when Tupelo and Lee Counties were both dry. A dry county meant that selling liquor there was illegal; several counties and states in the South were dry even after Prohibition ended.

Uncle Vester attends to Graceland's nativity display, December 1979.

A year after Vernon and his family moved to Memphis, Vester and his wife Clettes, who was Gladys's sister, followed. As the story goes—at least as it was always told by Vester—he showed a very young Elvis a few chords on the guitar. But Vester's greatest contribution to Elvis was his years as head gate guard at Graceland. From 1957 to his

Doshia Steele

One of the most interesting of Elvis's relatives in Tupelo was Doshia Steele, Mississippi's last widow of a Civil War veteran. Mrs. Steele was Jessie D. McClowell's sister, making her Elvis's great aunt. Elvis visited her at least once. He and his parents went to see her just before they moved to Memphis.

retirement in 1982, good-natured Vester manned the guardhouse by the famous Music Gates, and he became a favorite of fans. Charming, congenial, and always available for a photo, Vester was the perfect envoy for Elvis Presley and Graceland. Uncle Vester died on January 18, 1997.

Long after Elvis, Vernon, and Minnie Mae had died, Graceland still had a Presley in residence—Delta Mae Presley Biggs. One of Elvis's favorite relatives, Aunt Delta did not have children of her own, so she had doted on Elvis when he was a child, and Delta's husband, Pat Biggs, had always encouraged Elvis to pursue his goals and have faith in himself. Biggs died in 1966, and the following year, Elvis moved Aunt Delta to Memphis and put her on the payroll as a housekeeper and companion to her mother, Minnie Mae.

Delta was feisty and protective of Elvis. She was overtly mistrustful of his buddy bodyguards who were collectively known as the Memphis Mafia. She suspected that many were hangers-on who were only after the gifts he frequently bestowed upon them. Hotheaded and argumentative, Delta was known to give several of Elvis's buddies a piece of her mind, whether they deserved it or not.

Graceland was opened to the public in June 1982. Fans tramped across the grounds and through the first floor, marveling at the furniture, keepsakes, photos, and decor. In what must have been an awkward arrangement, the second floor and kitchen area were off limits to tourists, because Delta continued to live at Graceland. Hundreds of tourists and fans visited Elvis's home each day, with Delta going about her daily routine just above them. Whether by choice or request from Elvis Presley Enterprises, Delta did not show herself. After she died in 1993, the kitchen was included on the Graceland tour, and in 1998, most of the upstairs was opened for public viewing.

Other relatives who worked for Elvis included maternal cousins Junior and Gene Smith, who traveled with him when he toured. Junior, who had been disabled during the Korean War, died in 1961; Gene stayed with Elvis until the late 1960s, when he left after a disagreement. Elvis's uncles, Johnny and Travis Smith, were gate guards; cousins Billy and Bobby Smith served as personal aides. Patsy Presley, Elvis's first cousin and Vester and Clettes's daughter, began working as a secretary at Graceland in 1963. She befriended Priscilla and later married Elvis's chauffeur and valet, Marvin Gambill.

Many familiar stories, myths, and cherished memories swirl around the Presley clan, both in Tupelo and Memphis. Whether exaggerated or truthful, most of them emphasize just how close the family was.

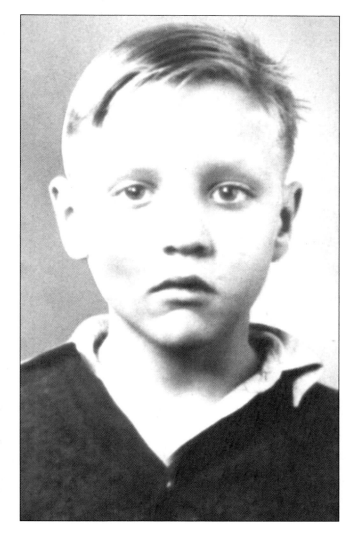

"I don't regard money or position as important. But I can never forget the longing to be someone. I guess **if you are poor,** you always **think bigger and want more** than those who have everything when they are born."

—ELVIS PRESLEY, *TIME*, MAY 7, 1965

Tupelo

- Tupelo was founded in 1859 and incorporated in 1870.

- Tupelo is named after the tupelo tree, which is a black gum.

- Tupelo National Battlefield is the site of the Battle of Tupelo, the last major battle fought in Mississippi during the Civil War.

- One of the deadliest tornadoes in history swept through Tupelo on April 5, 1936, killing 216 people.

- Tupelo is located along the Natchez Trace, a road that is older than America itself.

- In 1933, Tupelo became the first city to purchase power from the Tennessee Valley Authority (the TVA).

Myth vs. Fact

Legend has it that Elvis entered the talent contest at the **Mississippi–Alabama Fair and Dairy Show** in 1945 and won second place for singing "Old Shep." Made famous by Red Foley, the song is a ballad about a boy and his dearly departed dog. Elvis's prize supposedly consisted of free passes for the fair rides, plus five dollars. In very early versions of this story, Elvis was even said to have won the contest.

Research done by Bill Burk for his book *Early Elvis: The Tupelo Years* has dispelled this myth. A bespectacled Elvis did sing "Old Shep," but interviews with Tupelo residents and an old photo of the contestants (next page) reveal that the young boy did not win anything. At best, he may have placed fifth.

YOUNG DREAMS

As a child, Elvis knew all about poverty and struggle, yet his parents' love and his passion for music would see him through.

Located off a highway that transported locals between Tupelo and Birmingham, Alabama, and nestled among a group of rough-hewn homes along Old Saltillo Road, Elvis's birthplace was built by his father, Vernon, with help from Vernon's brother Vester and father, Jessie, whose relatively "spacious" four-room house sat next door. These were the humblest of beginnings. In the mid–1930s, in the middle of the Great Depression, East Tupelo was a home to poor sharecroppers and factory workers—as well as bootleggers and prostitutes—whose meager resources still largely outstripped those of Elvis's parents. Not only did Vernon and his wife rely on welfare to pay the $15 that Dr. William Robert Hunt charged for delivering Elvis and his stillborn twin brother, Jesse Garon, but neighbors and friends also had to provide them with diapers.

Confusion over the correct spelling of Elvis's middle name has existed since Dr. Hunt logged the name "Elvis Aaron Presley" in his ledger after the birth. The birth certificate issued by the state of Mississippi shows the spelling "Aron," which is also found on his draft notice. Elvis's gravestone in the Meditation Gardens at Graceland, however, is engraved with the more common spelling "Aaron." Alternate spellings of names were typical in the era of the Depression, particularly in rural communities where educational opportunities were limited and the written word was less significant than it is now. Since the Presleys chose Elvis's middle name to honor their friend and church songleader Aaron Kennedy, who was himself a twin, it is likely that "Aaron" was the intended spelling.

Before Elvis was born, Gladys earned $2 a day at the Tupelo Garment Company, while Vernon worked at various odd jobs, including one on the dairy farm of Orville S. Bean. With $180 that he borrowed from Bean after Gladys became pregnant in the spring of 1934, Vernon set about constructing a house, and he and Gladys moved in that December. Today, as part of a tourist attraction that includes a small museum, memorial chapel, gift shop, and wooded park on the renamed Elvis Presley Drive, the house that Vernon Presley built looks markedly different than when the future King of Rock 'n' Roll first tested his vocal cords there.

The two-room shotgun shack where Elvis was born has evolved from a modest dwelling to a major tourist attraction, complete with a museum, memorial chapel, and gift shop.

While the ceiling and roof of this Mississippi landmark have been replaced, the basic structure still stands, yet the wood exterior is now painted, the front porch has a swing, and the interior has been embellished with period furniture, wallpaper, curtains, and electrical appliances such as a sewing machine that the Presley family could never have afforded when they lived there. Forget the radio that now sits in the living room; the home was originally lit with oil lamps because it wasn't hooked up to the town's electric system. The nicely landscaped front yard is a far cry from the dirt patch where Gladys kept a flock of chickens and a cow.

Although material goods weren't readily available during his early years, Elvis never lacked the one thing that is most important to any child: the love of his parents. Vernon was a dedicated father and Gladys adored her only child, forming a bond that was so close, it extended to lifelong baby talk between the two, such as Elvis calling her by the pet name of Satnin'.

Scared to let him out of her sight, Gladys accompanied Elvis everywhere, including the tiny First Assembly of God Church, where her uncle Gains Mansell was the preacher and where Elvis got his first real taste of music. At age two, he would slide off his mother's lap, climb onto the platform in front of the 25-strong congregation, and stand before the choir, trying to sing along even though he was too young to know the words to the hymns.

Another place that mother and son regularly visited was the Priceville Cemetery, where Jesse Garon was buried in an unmarked grave. Although bolstered by Gladys's belief that, as reported in a September 1956 issue of *TV Guide*, "when one twin died, the one that lived got all the strength of both," Elvis grew up in his brother's shadow. Nevertheless, he was always mindful of Jessie's ghostly presence watching over him, ensuring that he tried to do the right thing. This, together with the special confidence he shared with his mother, encouraged an insular quality that Elvis would retain to the end of his days. Many who knew him, including his wife, Priscilla, have attested to a loneliness that no one could resolve, and while this side of Elvis was greatly exacerbated following Gladys's death during his early twenties, it stemmed from a childhood in which he often retreated into his own little world—a world defined by a strong attachment to his mother and the florid thoughts of his fertile imagination.

Life was fairly settled during Elvis's first three years. He and his parents formed a tight-knit trio, rarely socializing or venturing far from the family home—but everything changed in May 1938 after Vernon went to prison for his part in altering and cashing the check he received from Orville Bean.

This Presley family tombstone is located in Tupelo's Priceville Cemetery, where Elvis and his mother paid regular visits to the unmarked grave of his stillborn twin brother, Jesse Garon.

Vernon was sentenced to three years at the Mississippi State Penitentiary. He served only eight months of his sentence, but during that time Bean repossessed the Presley home, forcing Gladys and Elvis to move into a couple of temporary homes: next door with Vernon's parents, and then on Maple Street in Tupelo, where they lived with Gladys's cousins Frank and Leona Richards.

If this was a difficult period for Vernon, it wasn't much easier for his wife and son. Gladys struggled—and sometimes failed— to make ends meet taking in laundry and working as a seamstress, while Elvis suffered through the realization of the separation anxiety that he felt with regard to his father.

Elvis was extremely afraid of losing his father. When the family went swimming, Elvis didn't want Vernon to dive for fear that something bad would happen to him. In another instance, a neighbor's house caught fire, and Vernon rushed inside to help save their belongings. Gladys reportedly had to hold her distraught son back from going in after his father. Elvis cried and screamed at the possibility that Vernon could get hurt, and Gladys had to reassure him by telling him sharply to trust that Vernon knew what he was doing.

That last comment wouldn't have reassured the child in 1938, when many of his worst fears came true. His only respite came in the form of those weekends when Gladys and Elvis made the five-hour bus journey to visit Vernon in the Mississippi State Penitentiary at Parchman. The ten-hour round trip—which they made all in one day—presumably solidified the mother-son union more than ever.

When Vernon was released in February 1939, just a month after Elvis's fourth birthday, Gladys and Elvis were still living with Frank and Leona Richards on Maple Street. Before long, however, they were back in East Tupelo and, following a brief stay with Vester and Clettes, living in a succession of low-rent homes.

One of the few constants in Elvis's life around this time was the First Assembly of God Church, where he and his parents sang in the choir, as well as Lawhon Elementary

School on Lake Street, which he began attending in the fall of 1941. Already a loner, used to playing on his own more than with his few friends, Elvis soon learned to read, and he would while away hours on end with his small collection of comic books. He also became reacquainted with his father's absence. Benefiting from increased work opportunities created by America's entry into World War II, the Presleys relocated to the Mississippi Gulf Coast where Vernon and his cousin Sales found employment in the Moss Point Shipyard near Pascagoula in 1940. The relocation was short-lived. Missing their family and friends, Vernon and Gladys returned to East Tupelo about a month later.

Vernon spent most of 1942 living apart from his family in Mississippi, Alabama, and finally in Memphis, Tennessee, where he worked in a munitions plant while returning to East Tupelo to be with Elvis and Gladys on weekends.

"My daddy knew a lot of **guitar players,** and most of them **didn't work,** so he said, 'You should make up your mind to either be a guitar player or an electrician, but I never saw a guitar player that was worth a damn."

—ELVIS, FROM THE DOCUMENTARY
ELVIS ON TOUR, 1972

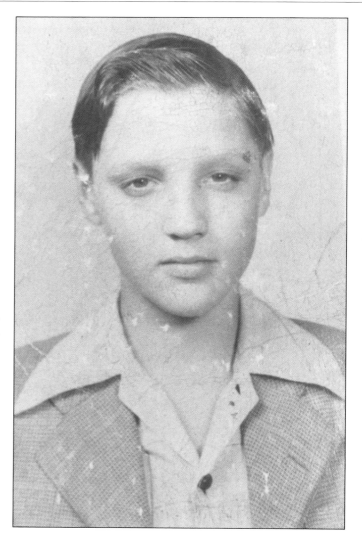

Even in elementary school, **Elvis** was attracted to girls and vice versa. His last **"romance"** before moving to Memphis was with Magdalene Morgan, who attended Lawhon Elementary School and the First Assembly of God Church with Elvis.

Mississippi Slim

Elvis learned about traditional country music from Mississippi Slim, whose real name was Carvel Lee Ausborn. Slim was a native of Tupelo and a fixture on local radio station WELO for more than 20 years. Elvis, who was friends with Slim's younger brother James, may have learned several guitar chords from Slim. Elvis's uncle Vester Presley also taught the young boy how to handle and play a guitar. It's possible that Elvis sang on WELO's amateur radio show called "Black and White Jamboree" (also known as "Saturday Jamboree"). Named for the Black and White hardware store, the Saturday afternoon program featured a live studio audience. Locals were allowed to perform on the program on a first-come, first-served basis. Elvis attended the show regularly, and he may have sung the traditional ballad "Old Shep" on the air when he was eight or nine.

In August 1956, after a visit to his barber, Elvis clowned around with one of Memphis's finest.

"We figured if we went to Memphis there would be **more money** and it would be **more fun** for Elvis, but in the early days we were bitterly disappointed. His mother and I walked the streets looking for work. We did this even in heavy rain or snow but for quite some time, there was no work to be found."

—VERNON PRESLEY

Elvis Lived Where?

370 Washington Street—the first Memphis address for the Presleys

572 Poplar Avenue

185 Winchester Street, Apartment 328—in a housing project called **Lauderdale Courts**

The Presleys lived in Lauderdale Courts from September 1949 to January 1953.

698 Saffarans Streeto

462 Alabama Street—Elvis lived
here when he first recorded at
Sun Studio

2414 Lamar Avenue

1034 Audubon Drive—the first house Elvis
bought after becoming a professional singer

3764 Elvis Presley Boulevard—**Graceland**

*Vernon and Gladys pose
proudly alongside their son's
growing fleet of cars at their
home on Audubon Drive.*

*For Elvis, Graceland was
much more than just a place
to live: It was the one place
where he could be himself
without a media frenzy.*

Elvis and his friends often went to the movies, and their favorite films were westerns. Here, **Elvis** displays his **quick draw.**

Elvis hangs out with his **closest friends,** who also lived
in Lauderdale Courts. From left: Farley Guy, Elvis, Paul Dougher,
and Buzzy Forbess.

L. C. Humes High School

- Elvis attended Humes High from 1949 to 1953.

- The school was named after Laurence Carl Humes, a former president of the Memphis Board of Education.

- In 1952, Elvis attempted to join the school's football team, the Tigers.

- The school's yearbook was called the *Herald.*

- On April 9, 1953, Elvis appeared in the school's annual Minstrel Show, though the program misspelled his name as "Elvis Prestly."

- The school later became a junior high called Humes Middle School.

Poplar Tunes

Poplar Tunes, founded by hardworking Joe Cuoghi, epitomizes the 1950s record shop. Located near Lauderdale Courts, the one-story brick building was a hangout for Elvis and his friends during their high school years. As a youth, Elvis purchased singles at Poplar Tunes to add to his ever-growing record collection. When he went from being a record collector to a recording artist, Poplar Tunes began selling his Sun singles. Most claim it was the first store to sell an Elvis Presley record. Because Elvis was from the neighborhood, his singles sold like wildfire, and he enjoyed signing autographs at the store for the local customers who supported him.

Elvis at Poplar Tunes

Elvis's Early Favorites

Gospel Music

Local gospel groups at Ellis Auditorium

Blackwood Brothers Quartet

Hovie Lister and the Statesman,
especially lead singer Jake Hess

Blues Music

Local performers at Green Owl
on Beale Street

Lowell Fulson at Club Handy
on Beale Street

Dewey Phillips's "Red Hot and Blue"
show on WHBQ

Arthur "Big Boy" Crudup

Arthur Gunter

Country Music

Eddy Arnold

Louvin Brothers (Gladys Presley's favorite)

Grand Ole Opry

Bob Neal's "High Noon Round-Up" show
on WMPS

Even as a teenager, Elvis had an impressive record collection.

Pop Music

Dean Martin

Mario Lanza

Elvis as a senior at Humes

"We talked about **getting jobs** when we got out of Humes; of **making a decent living.** Elvis always said he wanted a job where he could provide for his mother and father."

—Buzzy Forbess, Early Elvis: The Humes Years

Elvis's Early Resume

1950 Mowing lawns

1950 Loew's State Theater

1951 Precision Tool

1951 Loew's State Theater

1952 MARL Metal Products

1953 M.B. Parker Machinists

1953 Precision Tool

1954 Crown Electric

Loew's State Theater

At the Movies

According to accounts from his high-school friends, Elvis enjoyed going to the movies. The movies he saw included:

Tarzan

The ***Tarzan*** series, starring Johnny Weissmuller

City Across the River (1949), starring Tony Curtis, Stephen McNally, and Thelma Ritter

Samson and Delilah (1949), starring Victor Mature, Hedy Lamarr, and Angela Lansbury

Son of Ali Baba (1952), starring Tony Curtis and Piper Laurie

Houdini (1953), starring Tony Curtis and Janet Leigh

The Great Diamond Robbery (1953), starring Red Skelton - - - - - - - - - - - - - - -

The Blackboard Jungle (1955), starring Glenn Ford, Vic Morrow, and Sidney Poitier

East of Eden (1955), starring James Dean, Julie Harris, Jo Van Fleet, and Raymond Massey

Rebel Without a Cause (1955), starring James Dean, Natalie Wood, and Sal Mineo - - - - - -

Elvis was watching The Great Diamond Robbery when Dewey Phillips called him to WHBQ for his first radio interview.

Rebel Without A Cause

WDIA

WDIA radio went on the air for the first time in 1947 with a rotation of classical, pop, and country music. Each program was between 15 and 60 minutes, and the station broadcast only during the day. However, the station's owners, Bert Ferguson and John R. Pepper III, had always entertained the idea of reaching out to Memphis's African-American community, which constituted 40 percent of the city's population. In 1948, they hired Nat D. Williams, a former teacher and journalist, to host "Brown America Speaks," a program featuring prominent Black spokespersons and personalities. By October, WDIA was broadcasting music segments and other programs directed at Memphis's Black population, earning the nickname "the Mother Station of the Negroes." Local blues artist B. B. King hosted a musical segment and sometimes played his own music as well as that of other local rhythm-and-blues performers. Other programs featured gospel music.

The influence of blues and rhythm-and-blues on Elvis's music cannot be underestimated, and a source for that music was WDIA. The station is often remembered for its connection to Elvis's musical style. However, at the time, the station was far more important for the services it provided for the Black community. WDIA hosted musical events called "Goodwill Revues," and some of the ticket sales went to such charitable projects as the Goodfellows Christmas Basket Fund, summer baseball teams, and transportation for handicapped Black children to get to school.

BECOMING A STAR

A look back at the beginning of Elvis Presley's career offers a glimpse at a fascinating time in music history and an important era in American society. Elvis combined a variety of musical genres—blues, country, rhythm-and-blues—that exploded into an entirely new sound when they came pouring from his soul. Eventually dubbed "rockabilly," his music became one of the core sounds of rock 'n' roll. Not only was his music influential but his performing style, clothing choice, and hairstyle helped define a young generation eager to disassociate itself from past fashions and tastes. Not to be forgotten is the state of the pop music industry at the time, which was flexible enough to allow tiny record companies and regional radio stations to break new sounds with new artists.

Myth vs. FACT

On a Saturday afternoon late in the summer of 1953, eighteen-year-old Elvis Presley entered the **Memphis Recording Service.** Rock 'n' roll folklore holds that a naive young Elvis went to the studio that day to make a record for his mother's birthday. As late as 1968, an article by respected music critic Robert Hilburn repeated this apocryphal story. However, because Gladys Presley's birthday was April 25, the timing in this version of events does not add up. While no one knows for sure what prompted Elvis to go to the studio that day, one likely explanation paints him as being more ambitious than the Elvis folklore suggests. More than likely, Gladys's birthday was the last thing on his mind, because Elvis was looking to get discovered. He recorded "My Happiness" (originally by the Ink Spots) for his acetate, backed by "That's When Your Heartaches Begin."

Sun Studio/Memphis Recording Service

SPOTLIGHT ON

"I'll Never Stand in Your Way"

Elvis recorded this song in January 1954 on his second trip to the Memphis Recording Service. He hoped to attract the attention of Sam Phillips. On the back of this acetate is his version of "It Wouldn't Be the Same Without You."

"I'll Never Stand in Your Way," written by Fred Rose and Hy Heath, was well known at the time Elvis strolled through the door to make his second acetate. Joni James had enjoyed modest success with it in November 1953, and a few days after her record hit the stores, Ernie Lee released his version. "It Wouldn't Be the Same Without You" was recorded by country singer Jimmy Wakely during the 1940s.

ESSENTIAL SONGS

"HEARTBREAK HOTEL" VS. "DON'T BE CRUEL"

Two of Elvis's biggest hits from 1956—the year he became a national sensation in a mainstream market—reveal two different threads in his musical style.

The lyrics for "Heartbreak Hotel" were inspired by a newspaper story about a businessman who had committed suicide. "I walk a lonely street," read his suicide note, which spurred songwriter Tommy Durden to seek out publicist Mae Axton to cowrite

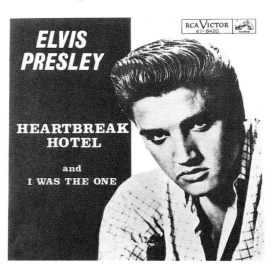

a song about alienation and abject despair. Axton offered the song to Elvis, and Elvis recorded it during his first session with RCA. Elvis rendered the song in a melodramatic style, reminiscent of pop singer Johnnie Ray, famous for his ballad "Cry." But the blues-tinged tone, aided by Scotty Moore's guitar breaks, Floyd Cramer's piano, and the magnified echo effect created a sense of desolation that was raw—like the blues.

"Don't Be Cruel," on the other hand, was influenced by pop music stylings, specifically those of Dean Martin from his 1955 hit "Memories Are Made of This." As smooth and fluid as "Hotel" is down and dirty, "Don't Be Cruel" reveals Elvis singing an up-tempo song with the Jordanaires nicely harmonizing as backup. Later, Elvis heard Black pop singer Jackie Wilson, a performer he greatly admired, sing "Don't Be Cruel" in Las Vegas. Wilson slowed down the pace, carefully enunciated the syllables of each lyric, and sang the last lines with flourish. Thereafter, Elvis's live performances of "Don't Be Cruel" usually offered a hint of Wilson's interpretation of the song.

Elvis poses with R&B singer Jackie Wilson after Wilson performed in Dick Clark's "Good 'Ol Rock 'n' Roll Review" at the Las Vegas Hilton, August 18, 1974. Elvis had been a big fan of Wilson's since the 1950s. When Wilson had a debilitating stroke in 1975, Elvis paid part of his medical expenses.

1956: A VERY GOOD YEAR

Sam Phillips sold Elvis's contract to nationally based RCA Records in November 1955. Recording for RCA gave Elvis exposure to mainstream audiences and primed him for television appearances on the major variety shows of the period, including *Tommy and Jimmy Dorsey's Stage Show*, *The Milton Berle Show*, *The Steve Allen Show*, and *The Ed Sullivan Show*. A television appearance in April attracted the attention of movie producer Hal Wallis, who signed Elvis to a contract. By the end of 1956, Elvis had conquered the major industries of show business—recording, television, and film.

This colorized publicity photo is of Elvis with a guitar in front of the RCA microphone. The original photo was taken in January 1956 at Elvis's first recording session for RCA. This photo was used to advertise a portable RCA record player that played singles.

Bill Burk: The Best Mythbuster

Bill Burk knew Elvis Presley for almost 20 years, and as a reporter for the Memphis Press-Scimitar, he wrote more than 400 newspaper stories and columns about him. He met and made friends with most of Elvis's associates and family, which gave him access to stories and photos that other publications did not have.

In 1980, while still reporting for the newspaper, Burk helped fan clubs that wanted to coordinate events for Elvis Week. In 1986, while working in public relations, he launched *Elvis World*, a Memphis-based newsletter for fans all over the world. Readers have included former president Bill Clinton, the late Raisa Gorbachev, former USSR premier Boris Yeltsin, President Robert Mugabe of Zimbabwe, and Japanese prime minister Junichiro Koizumi.

Burk has written more than a dozen books on Elvis. He prides himself on his accurate information and in printing rare stories and photos from people who, in many cases, have never spoken to the news media. In this capacity, Burk has debunked many myths about Elvis, painstakingly researching and printing the true version of events to the benefit of fans and scholars.

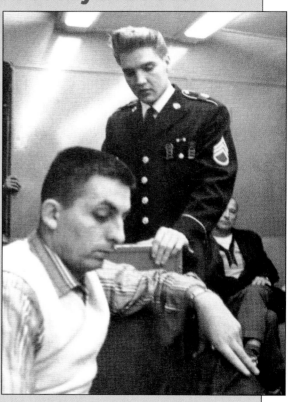

In March 1960, Bill Burk interviews Sgt. Elvis Presley in Memphis after his discharge from the army.

"ELVIS THE PELVIS"

Exactly where or from whom Elvis "borrowed" his legendary performing style for his live act has become another part of rock 'n' roll folklore. The truth is that his style, with its sensual hip movements and frenetic leg shaking, remains deceptively difficult to dissect. It was at once a hybrid of various influences as well as something unique to Elvis as an entertainer, something that differentiated him from other rockabilly or rock 'n' roll singers. Many biographers have claimed that Elvis's style was partly an influence from the flamboyant preaching style of Pentecostal ministers or the energetic performances of gospel singers Jake Hess and Jim Wetherington from the Statesmen. A witness to the musical developments on Beale Street from this era claims that Elvis got his wiggles from a Black musician named Ukulele Ike, who played the blues at the Gray Mule on Beale. Such claims, however, result from speculation and a desire to dissect his music; they cannot be substantiated.

During the 1950s, Elvis was asked about his performing style ad nauseam in interviews across the country. Every disc jockey, local reporter, and teenager working for her high school newspaper asked him about it, and he patiently and sincerely answered them. He repeatedly explained that his movements were the result of feeling the rhythm of the music. He was simply expressing his enjoyment of the music as he sang. While often acknowledging his respect for other singers and performers, as well as his debt to them, he rarely—if ever—mentioned any influence on his live act.

In a recorded interview intended as a supplement to a magazine, Elvis offered a thoughtful account of his performing style. He believed that his R&B-influenced music inspired him to release his nervous energy while he sang. And, if that excited his audiences, then they were all taking "something out of our system and no one gets hurt." Besides, he wanted to give his audiences a good show and let them know that he really enjoyed the music he was singing. Uncovering the sources of both Elvis's musical sound and his performing style is important in understanding why his music was so revolutionary, but it is significant that Elvis integrated those influences into a stunning style that was ultimately all his own.

At the beginning of his career, when he was a regional performer down South, little mention was made of his shakes and shimmies. Publicity and promotional material from the early period simply described him as a hot young country singer with a crazy new sound that drove the

Throughout 1956, the mainstream press grew increasingly insulting in their descriptions of Elvis's sensual performing style, often comparing it to a freak show or a striptease.

young audiences wild. It was only after Elvis began performing for mainstream television audiences in 1956 that his unique performing style created controversy.

Many reviewers for the national magazines and major newspapers got into the habit of comparing his live act to that of a stripper or burlesque dancer, implying that it was lewd or profane. As Tony Zoppie creatively reported in the *Dallas Morning News*, ".... the gyrating pelvic motions are best described as a cross between an Apache war dance and a burlesque queen's old-fashioned bumps and grinds."

Elvis often took the high road when pressed about these accusations and denunciations, but secretly they must have bothered him because his anger and pain occasionally slipped out during recorded interviews. In the August 1956 interview in *Lakeland*, reporter Paul Wilder brought up a column by Herb Rau of the *Miami News* in which Rau rabidly criticized Elvis and his fans. Rau called the singer a "no talent performer" and "the biggest freak in show business," and he described the singer's act as nothing but "pelvic gyrations" and "sex stimulations." Elvis countered by speculating that Rau was probably too old to have fun.

All the focus on his hips inspired some journalists to nickname the controversial singer "Elvis the Pelvis." The name infuriated Elvis, and he told reporter Paul Wilder and others that it was one of the most childish expressions he had ever heard from an adult. In retrospect, the controversy over his "gyrating hips" is often rendered in humorous tones or painted with a nostalgic brush. But the truth is that certain members of the press turned it into something quite ugly.

WHAT'S IN A NAME?

During the 1950s, Elvis was billed as:

The Hillbilly Cat

The Atomic-Powered Singer

The Freshest, Newest Voice in Country Music

The Nation's Newest Singing Sensation

The King of Western Bop

The King

By 1958, when no moniker was necessary, the posters simply proclaimed: He's Coming!

"We got this boy here from Humes High School, and **this is his first record,** and the first time we're playing it. **I want to see what y'all like about it.**"

—DEWEY PHILLIPS,
INTRODUCING "THAT'S ALL RIGHT," JULY 7, 1954.
HE WAS THE FIRST DEEJAY TO PLAY AN ELVIS RECORD.

SECRETS OF THE ROAD: 1954–1958

Almost as soon as his career began, Elvis took to the road with the Blue Moon Boys to promote their records. By the time Elvis went into the army in 1958, he had played almost every state in the union. The early years on the road comprise one of the least documented aspects of his career but also one of the most interesting. The era begins when Elvis was young, optimistic, and completely unknown, allowing fans a glimpse of an unguarded man enjoying his good fortune as a promising new singer.

Elvis, Scotty Moore, and Bill Black began by playing any local venue that would have them, including the Overton Park Shell, local clubs—even the openings of shopping plazas. Soon they were playing farther from home, driving long distances for one or two shows here and there. Regular appearances on Louisiana Hayride brought enough recognition for the group to join talented country-western stars on packaged tours. Some of the tours were set up by the Hayride, while others were organized by established promoters. These tours resulted in larger crowds, more venues, and the experience of working with an array of country music professionals ranging from established names to prominent newcomers. From 1954 to 1955, Elvis performed with country artists Bill Strength, Slim Whitman, Faron Young, Ferlin Huskey, Webb Pierce, the Wilburn Brothers, and Mother Maybelle and the Carter Sisters, plus up-and-coming stars such as Johnny Cash, Sonny James, and Charlie Feathers.

Elvis toured with country singer Bill Strength at least three times in 1955.

By 1956, when Elvis was exposed to a national audience, the crowds consisted mostly of teenage girls.

Elvis's music and performance style were decidedly different from traditional country, but he was a White singer from the South, and that automatically classified him as part of country music. Elvis always described himself as a spontaneous performer, naturally moving to the music, but the truth is that there was a measure of calculation in his performances. He exhibited an uncanny instinct for knowing what the fans wanted to see and hear. He teased them with a few hip and leg movements, they responded, and then he cut loose, singling out specific members of the audience to interact with. This phenomenon was reciprocal in nature, forming a strong bond between performer and audience.

Though he was notorious for attracting the affections of teenage girls during these years, the truth is that Elvis's look, music, and attitude also profoundly affected young men. He had a direct influence on aspiring singers such as Roy Orbison and Waylon Jennings, who saw him perform when they were teenagers in Texas during the mid-1950s. Orbison, who remembered Elvis from the Big D Jamboree in Dallas, recalled, "His energy was incredible, his instinct was just amazing . . . . There was no reference point in culture to compare it." Jennings was 17 years old when he met Elvis and Scotty Moore backstage in Lubbock, and they made a strong impression on the teenager after they launched into "Tweedlee Dee" for him and his friends.

His music and performing style were so high-powered that other artists had difficulty following his act. By mid-1955, Elvis and the Blue Moon Boys were carefully positioned on the roster so as not to detract from the other performers. Faron Young, who became friends with Elvis, eventually refused to go on after him, because he knew that part of the audience was only there to see this hot new singer. After Presley performed his three or four songs, they would either leave in droves or stand on their chairs and repeat, "Bring Elvis back," while other acts were on the stage. As Young told a promoter in Orlando, Florida, "I'm going on before Presley. That son of a bitch is killing the audience," which was show-business slang for the way a singer excited a crowd to the point where no other entertainer could satisfy them.

After Elvis became a national sensation in 1956, he toured less often on a roster with established country stars. He was deliberately disassociated from country music by the Colonel and Steve Sholes of RCA while the press affiliated him with rock 'n' roll, hounding him about "those pelvic gyrations." Elvis released several hit records in 1956, but his act continued to run only about 20 minutes, because the audiences could be contained for only that length of time before crowd control became a problem.

WHAT KIND OF MUSIC IS THIS?

When Elvis began his career, the press did not use the phrases "rock 'n' roll" and "rocka-billy" to describe music. Many had difficulty describing Elvis or his unique blend of musical genres. Some of their less-than-successful efforts include:

"rural rhythm" —*Memphis Press-Scimitar*

"His style is both country and R&B, and he can appeal to pop." —*Billboard*

"the R&B idiom of negro field jazz" —Robert Johnson, *Memphis Press-Scimitar*

"a boppish approach to hillbilly music" —*American Statesman*

"a hillbilly blues singer" —Charles Manos, *Detroit Free Press*

Vegas Flop

In April 1956, Elvis was booked into a two-week engagement at the New Frontier Hotel in Las Vegas, a venture that turned out to be a disaster. Perhaps he and his manager should have known better than to attempt to present Elvis in a major engagement outside the South with an audience made up mostly of adults— and no teenage girls. After a few performances, Elvis was bumped to second billing in favor of a more typical Vegas entertainer, comedian Shecky Green. Stung by the rejection, Elvis would remember his failure in Las Vegas for many years. One good thing did emerge from the Vegas trip, however. Elvis was introduced to "Hound Dog" when he saw Freddie Bell and the Bellboys perform the song in the hotel lounge. "Hound Dog" became Elvis's signature song in 1956, ultimately bringing him as much controversy as fame.

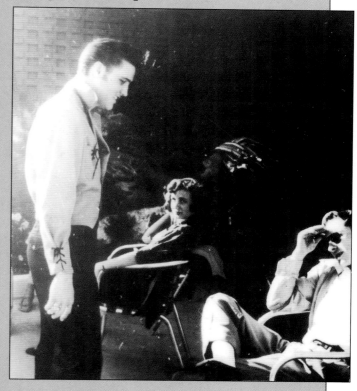

Elvis relaxes poolside at the New Frontier Hotel in Las Vegas in late April 1956.

SECRETS OF THE ROAD: 1970–1977

While Elvis's life on the road during the 1950s is relatively unknown, his concert tours of the 1970s are well documented by eyewitness accounts, newspaper stories, documentaries, and home movies by fans.

A typical Presley concert of the 1970s was more like a series of rituals and ceremonies than a performance by a mere entertainer. Making his entrance to Richard Strauss's *Also sprach Zarathustra*, popularly known as the "Theme from *2001*," Elvis charged into the spotlight as though propelled by some supernatural force. He incorporated karate kicks and tai chi arabesques into his act as well as other dramatic postures. Elvis also mocked his 1950s sex-symbol image by exaggerating the pelvic thrusts and sexual posturing of his old performing style, while making jokes about the "old days." More peculiar parts of his act included wiping the sweat from his brow and throwing the scarf or towel into the audience. This gesture became such a popular ritual that dozens of white towels were kept just offstage so that Elvis could throw them into the audience at frequent intervals. The most curious ritual of all was not performed by Elvis but by members of the audience. Each time Elvis played Las Vegas, the hotel stocked fresh undergarments in the restrooms because the women threw their underwear onto the stage while he was performing. Occasionally, they threw the keys to their hotel rooms.

One of the secrets of his successes during this decade was the illusion of intimacy that his onstage act conveyed. His rapport with his audiences was based on treating them like old friends or an extended family. Much interaction occurred onstage between Elvis and the audience members, such as the exchange of "gifts." Elvis threw towels and flowers into the audience; fans returned the gesture by throwing teddy bears, bouquets, and other mementos. Elvis kissed, hugged, and held hands with many of the women in the audience. They lined up just below the stage like a receiving line for royalty, waiting for the King to bless them with his touch. Audience members expected Elvis to sing specific songs and perform familiar moves; he always fulfilled those expectations.

This type of interaction can be traced back to Elvis's early career, when audiences became hysterical at his gyrations and performing style. If his fans were unusually loyal and demonstrative throughout his career, this interactive aspect of his act—from the beginning of his career to the end—was partially responsible.

Elvis sings "Love Me Tender" to the audience, mid-1970s. This song was the fans' cue to come down front to the stage to give flowers to Elvis, then kiss or hug him.

Sam Phillips

Born in 1923 and raised just outside of Florence, Alabama, Sam Cornelius Phillips was greatly influenced by his rural Southern roots. Working in the cotton fields, Phillips was exposed to gospel and blues music, and he experienced the poverty and hard life of many Depression-era families. As a record producer, he drew on those experiences to shape a new musical aesthetic—a purely Southern sound that combined rhythm-and-blues and country-western with a hardscrabble philosophy born of bad times. The music that emerged—a Dixie-fried sound called rockabilly—would emanate from Phillips's Sun Records in the mid–1950s and influence all of rock 'n' roll.

Phillips's genius lay in recognizing the talented singers and musicians of the region. Of his desire to record Southern-based music, Phillips reportedly mused, "I just knew this was culture, and it was so embedded in these people because of hardship . . . . Generation after generation, these people have been overlooked—black and white!" For his contribution in shaping modern music, Phillips was inducted into the Rock and Roll Hall of Fame.

Sam Phillips with Elvis

Marion Keisker

Any serious Elvis fan can tell you that Marion Keisker was working as a receptionist at Sun Studio the day Elvis came int to record his first acetate, but few know of Keisker's other accomplishments.

- Before working for the Memphis Recording Service/Sun Studio, Keisker was a Memphis radio personality on WREC, hosting a talk show called "Meet Kitty Kelly" among other programs.

- In 1955, while still working for Sun Studio, she returned to the air on WHER. The call letters were significant, because the station billed itself as "the Nation's First All-Girl Station." Keisker's voice was the first to be heard on WHER—just after midnight on Halloween, 1955, she gave the station's call letters, assigned frequency, and location.

- In 1957, a quarrel with Sam Phillips prompted her to quit her job and join the U.S. Air Force, where she received a commission. She eventually became a captain.

"...[Elvis] was like a mirror in a way: **whatever you were looking for, you were going to find in him.** It was not in him to lie or say anything malicious. He had all the intricacy of the very simple."

—Marion Keisker,
Last Train to Memphis
by Peter Guralnik

A BRAND-NEW SOUND

Elvis's first five records for Sun successfully integrated rhythm-and-blues with country and pop to produce rockabilly—one of the backbone sounds of rock 'n' roll.

1. "That's All Right" and "Blue Moon of Kentucky"
2. "Good Rockin' Tonight" and "I Don't Care If the Sun Don't Shine"
3. "Milkcow Blues Boogie" and "You're a Heartbreaker"
4. "Baby Let's Play House" and "I'm Left, You're Right, She's Gone"
5. "Mystery Train" and "I Forgot to Remember to Forget"

SPOTLIGHT ON

"That's All Right"

Elvis's first recording for Sun Records, "That's All Right," seemed to come about almost by accident. When Sam Phillips needed a singer to record a ballad called "Without You," he thought of Elvis Presley. Elvis had cut a couple of acetates at Phillips's Memphis Recording Service, and Phillips's assistant, Marion Keisker, had taped him for future reference. Phillips decided to let Elvis record "Without You," but the inexperienced singer wasn't able to master the song.

Elvis sang several other tunes for Phillips, who put him together with guitarist Scotty Moore for some seasoning. Moore, Elvis, and Bill Black were working together at Sun on the evening of July 5,

1954, trying to find a sound that clicked. Nothing seemed to be working. During a break, Elvis began singing Arthur "Big Boy" Crudup's country-blues tune "That's All Right" in a fast-paced, almost casual style. When Moore and Black jumped in, Phillips's voice boomed out from the control booth, "What are you doing?"

Phillips was excited by the trio's sound and recognized its potential. He recorded "That's All Right" that night and backed it a few days later with "Blue Moon of Kentucky." Elvis's approach to both songs differed from the originals. He used a more relaxed vocal style and higher key for "That's All Right" than Crudup had. He sped up the tempo for "Blue Moon of Kentucky" and omitted the high-pitched bluegrass singing style. Two elements were added to both songs that would make Elvis famous—syncopation and a "slapback" (electronically delayed) echo effect.

Arthur "Big Boy" Crudup

Dewey Phillips

Dewey Mills Phillips was a country boy from Adamsville, Tennessee, who came into his own on the airwaves of Memphis radio station WHBQ. One of the many jobs he held after he blew into town was at the Taystee Bread Bakery, where he was fired for talking the bakers into halting production of bread loaves in order to make little bread people. As an employee of Grant's dime store, he created a sensation by playing records and talking like a deejay over the store's intercom. He finally succeeded in talking his way onto the staff of WHBQ, which broadcast from the Hotel Chisca. Phillips took control of the 15-minute music program "Red Hot and Blue." Within a year, the show expanded to three hours a day, with Dewey often showcasing the music of local rhythm-and-blues artists. Phillips had no formal training in radio, but his jive approach to announcing made him appealing to audiences.

Dewey, who was a close friend to Sam Phillips but no relation, was the first deejay to play Elvis's "That's All Right." In fact, he played it over and over. So many requests for the record came into the station that Dewey interviewed Elvis on the air on July 7, 1955.

By the late 1950s, hard times set in for the one-of-a-kind deejay. Top 40 programming quickly became the mainstay of popular radio, and personalities like Dewey Phillips were shoved aside. In and out of work over the next dozen years, Phillips never regained the stature he enjoyed in the early 1950s. In 1968, he died of pneumonia at age 42.

Dewey Phillips, Wink Martindale, and Elvis

"While he appears with so-called hillbilly shows, Elvis's clothes are strictly sharp. His eyes are darkly slumbrous, his hair sleekly long, his sideburns low, and there is a lazy, sexy, tough, good-looking manner which bobby soxers like. Not all record stars go over as well on stage as they do on records. **Elvis sells."**

—ROBERT JOHNSON,
MEMPHIS PRESS-SCIMITAR,
FEBRUARY 5, 1955

"Some people **tap their feet,**
some people **snap their fingers,**
and some people **sway back and forth.**
I just sorta **do 'em all together,** I guess."

—ELVIS IN 1956, TALKING ABOUT HIS WAY OF MOVING ON STAGE

The musicians who backed Elvis were essential to his sound in the 1950s. Elvis, guitarist Scotty Moore, and bassist Bill Black were dubbed the **Hillbilly Cat and the Blue Moon Boys.** Moore and Black hitched their wagons to Elvis's star after recording "That's All Right" with him. Moore's driving guitar sound helped create Elvis's style, while Black's antics on his upright bass added humor and excitement to their live act. After appearing with the group on Louisiana Hayride,

drummer D. J. Fontana joined them on the road, although he never played on any of Elvis's Sun recordings. After Elvis became a household name, Moore, Black, and Fontana were not given the respect and salary they were due. Moore and Black split with Elvis in September 1957 over this issue. Both were wooed back, but things were never quite the same. Moore and Fontana recorded with Elvis after he returned from the army in 1960, but Black had already struck out on his own, enjoying moderate success with his own combo.

The "Memphis Kid" takes
a break during filming of
his second movie, Loving
You. *Elvis's character,
Deke–a truck driver
with a natural talent for
singing–was based on his
real-life experiences.*

ESSENTIAL CITY

JACKSONVILLE, FLORIDA

Jacksonville looms large in Elvis folklore for more than one reason. On May 13, 1955, Elvis performed at the Gator Bowl in front of 14,000 people, along with Grand Ole Opry stars Hank Snow, Faron Young, and members of the Carter Family. Since the girls in the audience were enthusiastic as usual, Elvis joked at the end of his set, "I'll see all you girls backstage." The girls took him at his word and pushed en masse through a gate that was accidentally left ajar. When they found him, they tore his pink shirt completely off his body, stole his shoes as he tried to escape to a shower stall, and went for his pants. Young and songwriter Mae Axton, among others, rescued him. Headlines

Elvis did six shows at the Florida Theater in Jacksonville, August 10–11, 1956. Judge Marion W. Gooding attended the first show and forced Elvis to tone down his act.

Elvis is in Jacksonville, Florida, in August 1956 on a date with a fan who won the "Win a Date with Elvis" contest from Hit Parader *teenzine.*

blared, "Girls Tear Clothes Off Elvis Presley," which influenced teenage girls everywhere to mob Elvis after his performances. The incident marked a turning point for Elvis in understanding both the positive and negative sides of fame.

The following year, on August 10, Elvis was ordered to "quieten his act" by Judge Marion W. Gooding while in Jacksonville. The order was in response to the criticisms of the singer's energetic performing style in which he gyrated his hips, thrust them forward, and then shook his body, which in turn provoked the girls into hysterics. Understanding the ridiculousness of the order, Elvis wiggled only his little finger during most of his shows. Once again, however, the publicity over the event made it a key moment in his career, because it added more fuel to the controversy over his performing style.

ESSENTIAL TV

BERLE VS. ALLEN

Elvis sings "Hound Dog" to an admirer on The Steve Allen Show.

commotion than any other single event in Elvis's career. For the climax of "Hound Dog," Elvis slowed down the tempo to repeat the song's chorus. While belting out this final verse to a blues beat, he turned his body in full profile and thrust his pelvis at the microphone. Elvis rested his hand next to the crotch of his pants, which emphasized the provocative connotation of the movement.

After the Berle show, Colonel Parker booked Elvis on *The Steve Allen Show*, a new comedy-variety program hungry for good ratings. Though Allen knew about the controversy generated by Elvis, he was also aware of the through-the-roof ratings. The savvy comedian successfully diffused Elvis's sensuality by making him part of the comedy of the show. Elvis's appearance in a tuxedo singing to a sad-eyed basset hound plopped down on a pedestal is almost as famous as his notorious performance on Berle's program.

The television appearance that generated the most controversy was when Elvis appeared on *The Milton Berle Show* on June 5, 1956. His highly charged performance of "Hound Dog" had contributed to more

THE ED SULLIVAN SHOW

No TV appearance has contributed so much to the Elvis Presley legend as *The Ed Sullivan Show*, primarily because of the decision to show Elvis only from the waist up during his performance of "Heartbreak Hotel" and "Hound Dog." Even nonfans know this tidbit of Elvis lore. Much, however, has been exaggerated about this event. The truth is that the order came during Elvis's *third* appearance on Sullivan's show. How much Sullivan had to do with the decision is unknown.

LET'S DANCE

"JAILHOUSE ROCK"

Elvis's performance of the title song from his third film is so iconic that it is seldom discussed from a fresh angle. It is a potent symbol of Elvis in the prime of his early career as a rockin' rebel raging against the chains of the system. Again, folklore colors many of the facts surrounding this performance.

For decades, books claimed that Elvis himself choreographed the dance, but that isn't quite an accurate account of what happened. It was choreographer

Elvis is having a blast during the shooting of "Jailhouse Rock." The film was released on November 8, 1957.

Alex Romero who was in charge of the big production number for "Jailhouse Rock." At first, he worked out some traditional dance steps for Elvis along the lines of Gene Kelly, but it quickly became apparent that these did not suit the young rocker's style. Romero then asked Elvis to play a few of his records and move naturally to them. After studying Elvis's performing style, the choreographer went home and worked out a different routine based on Presley's pelvic gyrations, knee jerks, and other signature moves. The next day, he and Elvis rehearsed the new dance, which the singer quickly picked up.

Elvis may have contributed to this well-known production number, but he did not officially choreograph it.

The set for the number was a simple scaffolding with barred doors; it was so minimalist that it was almost abstract, which differed from the more naturalistic settings of most of his production numbers throughout his film career. The result is a more timeless look to the set design, compared to the time-bound nature of most of his movie musical numbers.

This publicity photo was released to teenzines and fanzines in 1956.

"It was bedlam onstage. The noise was so loud we couldn't hear him play; we had to watch him. D. J. [Fontana], being an old burlesque drummer, could follow Elvis and take cues from his body motions and get us through it."

—Scotty Moore

From left are D. J. Fontana, Scotty Moore, Bill Black, and Elvis. They are poolside at the New Frontier Hotel in Las Vegas, April 1956.

ELVIS AND THE GIRLS

"It didn't matter what he did [onstage]. He would act silly or say something silly—get the words wrong or make up words. He just couldn't do anything wrong . . . . I learned since—it was because he really loved his audience. He loved his fans more than anybody I've ever seen."

—WANDA JACKSON, COUNTRY SINGER

"At Russwood Park, Elvis was the primary entertainer . . . . The girls threw apartment keys to him. I'm not lying to you. They were screaming, and they would actually pull out their own hair."

—BILL PERRY, ELVIS'S NEIGHBOR IN LAUDERDALE COURTS

THE GOLD LAMÉ SUIT

Hollywood clothing designer Nudie Cohen created the famous gold suit for Elvis for his 1957 tour. The suit consisted of gold lamé slacks and a jacket woven from spun gold thread, but Elvis disliked it because it was heavy and uncomfortable. The pants ripped during the tour, and Elvis never wore the entire suit again, though he does appear in full lamé splendor on the cover of the 1959 album *50,000,000 Elvis Fans Can't Be Wrong: Elvis' Gold Records, Vol. 2*. The suit is so well known that it has become an icon of the King's early years, and it was lampooned by rival Pat Boone on a 1964 album cover.

ESSENTIAL ALBUMS

ELVIS PRESLEY VS. *ELVIS IS BACK!*

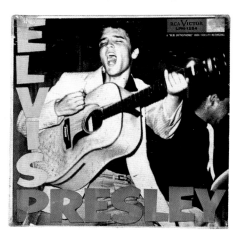

Elvis Presley was the singer's first album, which was released by RCA Records, not Sun. Moving to RCA meant going national and international in promotion and distribution. Steve Sholes, RCA's premier A&R (artist and repertoire) man, had helped sign Elvis, and he was aware that the execs were closely watching this unusual new artist who did not fit into any of the company's existing categories of music.

Elvis did not read music, nor did he have any professional experience arranging it. But he had an instinctive approach to recording, in which he sang, played it back, discarded it, and then sang another take. Thus, Sholes watched Elvis during his first recording session on January 10 and 11, 1956, with a certain amount of trepidation. But Sholes and RCA need not have worried, because *Elvis Presley* sold more than 360,000 copies in about six weeks. The career of RCA's most famous artist was launched.

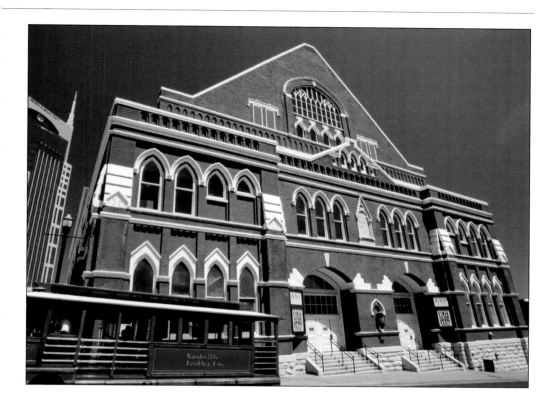

In the fall of 1954, Elvis was invited to perform on the **Grand Ole Opry.** On October 2, the Hillbilly Cat and the Blue Moon Boys drove from Memphis to Nashville to appear on the South's biggest and brightest stage. The audience, however, was not exactly enthusiastic. Because the Opry had always been a bastion of traditionalism, and reluctant to accept many changes in country music, including the use of electric guitars and drums, it's not surprising that Elvis's highly charged performance of blues-inspired music was not met with much appreciation.

"Maybe it's ironic that after that first appearance [on the Grand Ole Opry] the head of the Opry suggested that **Elvis try to find a day job,** and that Elvis cried all the way to Memphis after the Opry show. Then he went on to **become the biggest star** since Hank Williams. There's some kind of justice in that, I think."

—HANK WILLIAMS, JR.,
REPRINTED IN *ELVIS! THE LAST WORD,* 1991

On the Road, 1954–1955

Elvis appeared with a variety of country-western acts while under contract to Sun. Though his music did not sound like country, it was logical for him to tour the country circuits throughout the South. He toured with several singers who would become country music's biggest performers in the 1950s and 1960s, including Johnny Cash, Faron Young, Ferlin Huskey (later Husky), the Wilburn Brothers, Mother Maybelle and the Carter Sisters, Sonny James, Hank Locklin, Hank Snow, Webb Pierce, and the Louvin Brothers.

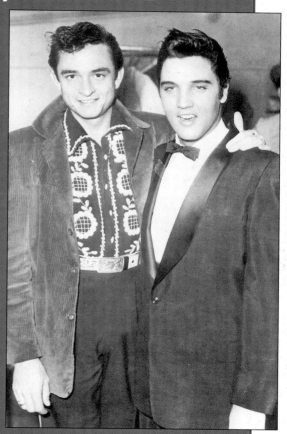

Johnny Cash with Elvis

"This cat came out in red pants and a green coat and a pink shirt and socks, and **he had this sneer on his face** and he stood behind the mike for five minutes, I'll bet, before he made a move. Then he hit his guitar a lick, and he broke two strings. So there he was, these two strings dangling...and these high school girls were **screaming and fainting** and running up to the stage, and then he started to move his hips real slow like he had a thing for his guitar."

—COUNTRY SINGER BOB LUMAN

ELVIS'S HAIR

Outside of his music and performing style, the single most controversial aspect about Elvis Presley was not his Southern background, his night life, or even his love life—it was his hair! From the ducktail and sideburns at the beginning of his career to the blue-black locks of the 1970s, the amount of attention paid to his hair bordered on a national fixation.

Elvis's ducktail haircut is clearly visible in this photo taken in Las Vegas in May 1956.

In 1956, when rock 'n' roll was under fire across most of the country, the popular press not only skewered Elvis for his music and sensual performing style, but they also ridiculed him for anything that drifted too far from familiar mainstream tastes. He was maligned for his Southern accent, his lack of decorum, and his flashy clothes, but, most of all, they were severely critical of his long sideburns and ducktail haircut, which was so heavily laden with pomade that his blond hair looked black. Elvis's hairstyle was criticized because of its length, his use of pomade, and the fact that so many teenagers emulated it. His sideburns and ducktail haircut became a symbol of everything that made him different—and therefore threatening. To ridicule his hair was a defense against that threat.

Despite the criticisms, Elvis was proud of his hair, spending a lot of time grooming it for the right effect. While touring with Elvis in 1955, Jimmie Rodgers Snow looked on in amazement every morning as the nation's newest singing sensation combed his hair. Elvis used three different hair aids to get the effect he wanted. For the front, he used butch wax, a strong pomade designed for butch haircuts, and for the sides and back, he used two separate hair oils. He liked the sides to stay in place when he sang, but he wanted the front to fall in front of his face when he moved provocatively, because the effect made the girls scream.

Elvis's natural color was dark blond, though he made it look much darker. Shortly after finishing the film *Loving You*, he dyed his hair black, which became a permanent choice. Over the years, friends and biographers have speculated as to why Elvis preferred black hair: Some claim that he wanted his hair to match his mother's, whose own tresses were dyed black; others remember him saying that dark hair made his blue eyes stand out. More than likely, the color just appealed to him.

From 1956 to 1958, the constant focus on his hair made it part of his image as the rebellious rock 'n' roller and potent sex symbol. No wonder when the Army shaved off his hair in March 1958, the press was there to photograph every chunk of hair

Elvis is inducted into the Army, March 24, 1958. Reporters were allowed to record the day's events, including the shearing of his famous ducktail haircut.

"THE MOST ICONIC HAIRSTYLE"

Thirty years after his death, Elvis's hair is still distinctive. In a 2006 British poll taken by Argos, Presley's hair was voted "the Most Iconic Hairstyle Ever." The Beatles' famous mop tops were voted #4.

that fell from his head. In 1960, when he resumed his career after his stint in the Army, the Colonel, producer Hal Wallis, and his Hollywood agent decided that a more mature, well-groomed image was needed for Elvis to steer him away from controversy and to gain acceptance by the mainstream audience. Appropriately, his ducktail haircut never grew back.

CLOTHES MAKE THE MAN

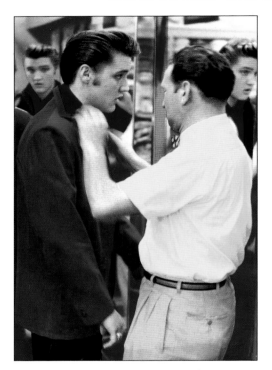

Bernard Lansky fits his most famous client in Lansky's Clothing Emporium at 126 Beale Street.

Many of the candid photos of Elvis onstage or with fans from the 1950s are in black and white. If they were in color, they would reveal another reason why the press found Presley so strange. More than likely, he was wearing a kelly green jacket with bright blue pants, or a red satin shirt with a loud tie, or white buck shoes with red heels, or some variation of pink and black.

Elvis's taste in clothes are part of his myth, and every fan knows that during his early career, he purchased many of them at Lansky Bros. on Beale Street in Memphis. Owned and operated by Bernard and Guy Lansky, the store began as an Army surplus store after World War II but evolved into a clothing store that catered to African-American R&B artists and white rockabilly singers. Most of the outrageous attire that surprised the press in the mid-1950s undoubtedly came from Lansky's.

Elvis bought at least one of his high-school prom suits at Lansky's, and Bernard was the one who fitted him for it. The circle was closed in 1977 when Lansky's provided the suit that Elvis was buried in. Bernard made the white burial suit especially for him, accented by a white tie. In a simple but touching comment, the old clothier remarked, "I put his first suit on him, and I put his last suit on him."

One suit that Elvis did not purchase at Lansky's was the legendary gold jacket and slacks woven from spun gold thread, with a matching string tie and white ruffled shirt.

Elvis asked the famed Hollywood clothing designer Nudie Cohen to create this special suit for him for his 1957 tour across the northern United States and parts of Canada. Critics and journalists responded to Elvis in his gold suit like bulls to a red flag. Along each leg of the tour, newspapers never failed to mention the legendary gold tuxedo. Though other entertainers, particularly Liberace, could wear outrageous costumes without criticism, Elvis was always ridiculed or criticized.

A taste for sartorial splendor also marked Elvis's image during the 1970s, when he returned to the stage to perform before live audiences. The jumpsuits, which were designed by Bill Belew, were an original touch to his act that became iconic of this era, though they have since been appropriated by impersonators and turned into a ridiculous stereotype of Elvis. Belew designed some of Elvis's offstage wardrobe, which often included accents like high collars, open necks, multicolored scarfs, and colorful shirts. Elvis liked to accessorize with canes, capes, jewelry, and oversize jeweled sunglasses.

LANSKY'S RECYCLED

The building that used to house Lansky's on Beale Street has been used by many organizations and businesses over the years, including the Center for Southern Folklore and EP's Memphis Restaurant. In 2006, Memphis restauranteur Jimmy Ishii opened the EP Delta Kitchen and Bar in Lansky's former location.

Elvis's personal taste in clothing and accessories was never ordinary.

"Why buy a cow when you can get milk through the fence?"

—Elvis, when asked if he would marry, "Teener's Hero," *Time*, May 14, 1956

"Baby Let's Play House"

Elvis's fourth single for Sun Records, recorded on February 5, 1955, and released in late April, became his first effort to chart nationally. Backed by "I'm Left, You're Right, She's Gone" on the flip side, "Baby Let's Play House" stayed on Billboard's country chart for ten weeks, reaching number ten.

Rhythm-and-blues singer Arthur Gunter wrote and recorded the song in 1954, basing it on country singer Eddy Arnold's 1951 hit, "I Want to Play House with You." A rhythm-and-blues reworking of a country-western song, "Baby Let's Play House" was perfect for Elvis's rockabilly repertoire. Gunter himself had been influenced by rockabilly artists, and he made a good model for Elvis, who had purchased a copy of Gunter's version the previous December at the House of Records in Memphis. Elvis made the song his own with the inclusion of the syncopated phrasing "Babe-babe-baby" in the verse. He also tinkered with the lyrics, changing "You may have religion" to "You may drive a pink Cadillac"—a humorous foretelling of the car he would come to be identified with. Sam Phillips added drums to the recording session for the song, marking the first time drums were used on an Elvis Presley single.

THE FRESHEST, NEWEST VOICE IN COUNTRY MUSIC

ELVIS PRESLEY

"Howdy to all my friends at the Jimmie Rodgers Memorial"

Featuring His Latest Hit

"YOU'RE RIGHT, I'M LEFT, SHE'S GONE"
b/w
"BABY, LET'S PLAY HOUSE"
SUN-217

DJ— Free sample by writing to Bob Neal, 160 Union Ave., Memphis, Tenn.

For available dates

Featured Star, KWKH Louisiana Hayride

WRITE WIRE PHONE | BOB NEAL Exclusive Personal Management 160 Union Ave., Memphis, Tennessee Phone: Office 8-3667 ● Home 4-4029

The Colonel

- Tom Parker was born Andreas Cornelis van Kuijk in Breda, Holland.

- Parker first saw Elvis in the spring of 1955 when Elvis was booked on a tour with country singer Hank Snow. The Colonel operated Snow's Jamboree Attractions.

- Parker's title of Colonel was not a military rank but an honorary title, which was bestowed on him by the state of Louisiana in 1953. In 1955, he was made an honorary Colonel of Tennessee.

- As a young man, Parker worked as a carnival barker and performer. Legend has it that as a carny, he painted sparrows yellow and sold them as parakeets.

- Elvis and the Colonel signed their first contract in August 1955, though Bob Neal was Elvis's official manager. By March 15, 1956, Neal was completely out of the picture, and the Colonel was Elvis's sole manager.

"People say the Colonel has a **good thing in me.**
Sure he has. And I've got a **good thing in him.**"

—ELVIS

"I'd rather try and **close a deal with the devil.**"

—FILM PRODUCER HAL WALLIS COMMENTING ON THE COLONEL

When Elvis charged in front of the cameras for the first time on

Tommy and Jimmy Dorsey's *Stage Show*

on January 28, 1956, he began a love-hate relationship with the television industry that kept his name in the headlines for most of that year. He returned to *Stage Show* on February 4, February 11, February 18, March 17, and March 24.

Rock 'n' roller Elvis and big-band leaders Tommy and Jimmy Dorsey represented popular music from two different eras.

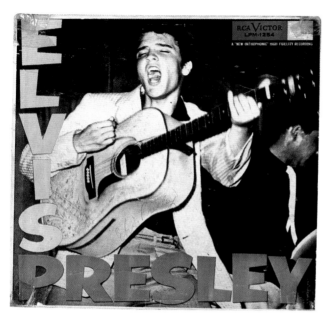

Released on March 13, 1956, *Elvis Presley* sold more than 360,000 copies by the end of April. At $3.98 per album, this made it **RCA's first million-dollar album** by a single artist. *Elvis Presley* also became the first album in music history to sell more than a million copies. It reached No. 1 on Billboard's Top LPs chart.

ELVIS PRESLEY

Side One
Heartbreak Hotel
I Was The One
Blue Suede Shoes
I'm Counting On You
I Got A Woman
One-Sided Love Affair
I Love You Because
Just Because
Tutti Frutti

Side Two
Trying To Get To You
I'm Gonna Sit Right Down And Cry (Over You)
I'll Never Let You Go (Little Darlin')
Blue Moon
Money Honey
Shake, Rattle And Roll
My Baby Left Me
Lawdy, Miss Clawdy
I Want You, I Need You, I Love You

Compilation Produced by
Ernst Mikael Jørgensen and Roger Semon
Original Engineer: **Sam Phillips,
Bob Ferris and Ernie Oelbrich**
Executive Directors: **Mike Omansky
and Klaus Schmalenbach**
Project Director: **Dalila Keumurian**

Elvis Presley zoomed into big-time entertainment practically overnight. Born in Tupelo, Mississippi, Elvis began singing for friends and folk gatherings when he was barely five years old. All his training has been self-instruction and hard work. At an early age, with not enough money to buy a guitar, he practiced for his future stardom by strumming on a broomstick. He soon graduated to a $2.98 instrument and began picking out tunes and singing on street corners.

After earning some money by working at part-time jobs, Elvis walked into a small recording company studio and asked to make a record, at his own expense. In a few months his first record was released and became an overnight sensation. Following his graduation from high school, Elvis began an extended round of personal appearances and then signed his contract with RCA Victor. The rest is history.

Elvis is the most original protagonist of popular songs on the scene today. His style stands out vividly on records and in personal appearances and accounts for the universal popularity he has gained.

RCA is a registered trademark of General Electric Company, USA. ℗2000 BMG Entertainment. The copyright in this sound recording is owned by BMG Entertainment. All label copy and stamp scans © 2000 The RCA Record Label. Distributed by the BMG Company. All trademarks and logos are protected. Made in the EU(UK).

"I lose myself in my singing. Maybe it's my early training singing gospel hymns. I'm **limp as a rag,** worn out when a show's over."

—ELVIS,
TACOMA NEW TRIBUNE,
SEPTEMBER 2, 1957

"He's just one big hunk of **forbidden fruit.**"

—Teenage girl to songwriter Mae Boren Axton

"In a pivoting stance, his hips **swing sensuously** from side to side and his entire body takes on a **frantic quiver,** as if he had swallowed a jackhammer."

—*TIME*, MAY 15, 1956

THE JORDANAIRES

This gospel quartet has backed a diverse range of performers since it was formed in 1948, including Kitty Wells, Hank Snow, and Ricky Nelson. The group's lineup has changed several times over the years. The four men who backed Elvis Presley were Hoyt Hawkins (baritone), Gordon Stoker (first tenor), Hugh Jarrett (bass), and Neal Matthews (second tenor). In January 1956, Stoker was included as a backup singer on Elvis's first RCA recording session in a makeshift group with Ben and Brock Speer of the gospel-singing Speer Family. On another session later that year, Stoker was again hired to back Elvis without the rest of the quartet. When Elvis asked where the rest of the Jordanaires were, Stoker replied that he had been the only one asked. Elvis reportedly told him, "If anything comes of this, I want the Jordanaires to work all my sessions from now on, and my personal appearances, too." With that verbal agreement, the Jordanaires became "the Sound Behind the King" for more than a decade.

Graceland

- Graceland was built in 1939 by Dr. Thomas Moore and named after his wife's aunt, Grace Toof.

- Elvis purchased Graceland in March 1957 for slightly more than $100,000. The house was located on 13.8 acres of land.

- After the purchase, Elvis renovated the house and then made several additions over the years until Graceland consisted of 23 rooms, and the grounds included the Trophy Room and Meditation Garden, as well as a carport, bath house, and racquetball court.

- Graceland was opened to the public in 1982 and placed on the National Register of Historic Places in 1991.

Above: Elvis in Las Vegas, 1956.
Inset: Elvis mugs in a 25-cent photo booth.

"When I first knew Elvis, he had a **million dollars worth of talent**. Now he has a million dollars."

—Colonel Tom Parker, 1956

"My fans **want my shirt,** they **can have my shirt.** They put it on my back."

—ELVIS, *ILLUSTRATED,* SEPTEMBER 7, 1957

Otis Blackwell

Respected singer-songwriter Otis Blackwell composed many rock 'n' roll standards in the 1950s and 1960s. Born in Brooklyn in 1932, Blackwell grew up admiring country-western singer and actor Tex Ritter. He became a staff writer for Shalimar Music in early 1956 after he sold six songs, including "Don't Be Cruel," for $25 each to that company. Blackwell had been standing in front of the Brill Building (home to rock 'n' roll music publishing) in New York City on Christmas Eve when an arranger asked him if he had any songs to sell. The man then took Blackwell to meet Shalimar's owners, who purchased the songs and hired him after the holidays. Elvis recorded ten Blackwell compositions, including "Fever" (written with Eddie Cooley), "All Shook Up," "Paralyzed," and "Return to Sender" (cowritten with Winfield Scott). Among Blackwell's other rock 'n' roll classics are Jerry Lee Lewis's "Great Balls of Fire" and "Breathless." Blackwell sang on the demos of his songs for Elvis and Jerry Lee and imitated their styles, but he and Elvis never met.

"I'll **not have him at any price—** he's not my cup of tea."

—Ed Sullivan before Elvis's ratings-busting performance on *The Steve Allen Show*, July 23, 1956

"I want to say to **Elvis Presley** and the country that **this is a real decent boy,** and we've never had a pleasanter experience on our show with a big name than we've had with you."

—Ed Sullivan after Elvis's third appearance on *The Ed Sullivan Show*, January 6, 1957

Best Elvis Collectibles: 1950s

Elvis Presley Lipsticks. Merchandiser Hank Saperstein made a deal with the Colonel to market Elvis's image on about 30 products, including lipstick. Shades included Hound Dog Orange, Heartbreak Pink, Cruel Red, and Tutti Frutti Red.

Elvis Presley Sneakers. Two different colors of sneakers were available, a green and black pair and a black and white pair.

Elvis Presley Underwear. After the Saperstein deal, fans could literally dress themselves from head to toe in Elvis, but the underwear must have generated the most interest.

Teddy Bear Perfume. Teen-Age, Inc., came up with Teddy Bear Eau de Parfum, inspired by Elvis's 1957 hit single "Teddy Bear." The tall, slender bottle featured a photo of Elvis from the 1950s. Collectors should beware of the reissue from the 1960s, which features a later photo of Elvis.

The Pink Items. In 1956, Elvis Presley Enterprises issued an autograph book, diary, scrapbook, photo album, and record case as a set of must-have accessories for every teenage girl. All of the items were dusty pink and featured the same black line drawing of Elvis.

Teenzines

Among the most delightful of all magazines about Elvis are the teenzines from the mid-to-late 1950s, because they cover the burgeoning days of rock 'n' roll. One of the most sought-after single-issue magazines is *Elvis Presley: Hero or Heel?* Another is *Elvis Answers Back*, which included a 78 rpm flexi disc recording with Elvis's voice. Regularly issued teenzines of the era included *Dig* and *Hep Cats*.

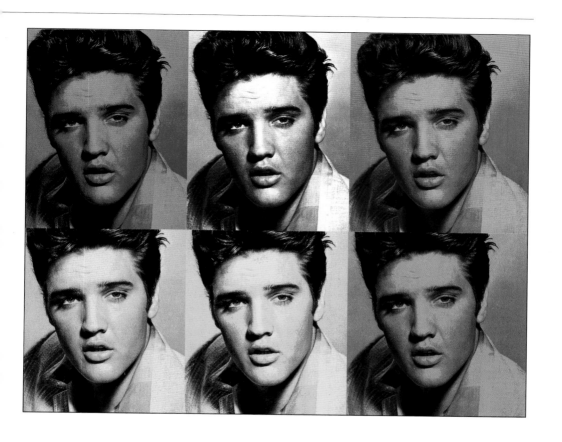

"**Before Elvis,** everything was in black and white. Then came Elvis. Zoom, **glorious Technicolor.**"

—Keith Richards

CRAZY ABOUT GIRLS

If Elvis could not leave the girls alone, then the reverse was also true. From fans to friends to femme fatales, women were an important part of the Elvis Presley story throughout his career, whether he was the dangerous rock 'n' roller, the handsome leading man, or the famous superstar.

Long after talent coordinator Horace Logan worked with Elvis Presley on the legendary radio program Louisiana Hayride, he recalled, "[Elvis] was absolutely crazy about girls. He loved them—both figuratively and literally . . . . During that period in his life, I never saw Elvis take an alcoholic drink . . . . I never saw him take so much as a puff from a regular cigarette, much less a marijuana cigarette. But he had an insatiable addiction to girls."

TEENAGER IN LOVE: DIXIE, JUNE, AND ANITA

Much has been written about Elvis's teenage years in Memphis, some fact and some fiction. Part of the appeal of this phase of his life is that it allows a glimpse at an unspoiled young man who liked to bring home his best girl to meet his parents.

His first serious girlfriend was probably Dixie Locke—who had the perfect name for a nice Southern girl. The trajectory of their romance is like a walk back in time: She noticed Elvis at her church in 1953 when she was about 15; she spoke to him for the first time at a roller rink; they went to the movies on their first official date; she wore his class ring when they went steady; he escorted her to her high-school prom. Gladys Presley liked Dixie, and her family accepted Elvis, even though they found his mode of dress odd. Elvis and Dixie attended the Assembly of God Church, occasionally went to Reverend Brewster's African-American church to hear the music, and frequented the monthly All-Night Singings at Ellis Auditorium. The common denominator of these activities was gospel music, which both of them enjoyed immensely.

The young couple talked seriously about getting married, but Dixie soon had a rival for Elvis's affections—his career in the music industry. When Elvis recorded his first commercial single for Sun Records, the end of their relationship was inevitable. Her path toward a normal life, including marriage, family, and a home, was no longer his path.

After he began to tour to promote his Sun recordings in 1954 and early 1955, Dixie and Elvis drifted apart. Though he would call her while he was on the road, worried that she wouldn't be there for him

Elvis leans against the green Lincoln, which Vernon bought for him when he was a high-school junior.

when he returned, he was seeing other girls while he was touring. Dixie found it difficult to fit in with his new friends, whom she found coarse and wild. When he berated her for going out on the weekends with her girlfriends instead of staying at home, she knew he was being unreasonable. They broke up in the summer of 1955; Dixie married a year later, fulfilling her dream just as Elvis was fulfilling his.

Elvis met June Juanico at a concert at Keesler Air Force Base in 1955 during her namesake month of June. Juanico had made eye contact with Elvis while he was performing, and during the intermission, she deliberately went to the ladies' room so she could walk by him. Elvis reached through the crowd of people surrounding him and grabbed her arm as she strolled by. He asked her to stay for his second set so that the two could go out afterward. June and Elvis hit it off and drove around Biloxi, Mississippi, for most of the night talking and getting acquainted. A year later, June visited him in Memphis, and they picked up where they had left off. June met Elvis's parents, feeling right at home with Gladys.

The next month, Elvis arrived in Biloxi to start a vacation, though his arrival was a surprise to June. They dated steadily for three weeks, which was the most prolonged span of time that they would spend together; the relationship was not on the

same level as Elvis and Dixie's. If the press had not gotten wind of their romance, June Juanico might not be remembered today. Because the press rushed to print a story that the pair was engaged, June and Elvis jumped into a car and drove to New Orleans, where Elvis appeared on radio station WNOE to dispel the rumors in person. According

Elvis hugs June Juanico, whom he dated in 1955 and 1956. June later wrote about her romance with Presley in Elvis: In the Twilight of Memory.

to June, Elvis had promised Colonel Tom Parker that he would not do anything detrimental to his career for three years, including getting married, engaged, or even tied down with a girlfriend.

A month later while touring with Elvis in Florida, June answered a few questions from a reporter. She innocently admitted that she loved Elvis, while acknowledging that he was married to his career. Parker exploded with anger when he read the paper and demanded in front of the humiliated June that Elvis "do something about this." Later, Elvis did damage control by declaring to another reporter that he had 25 girls that he dated regularly, and June was just one of them. A few days later when June's mother was interviewed and spilled the beans about the seriousness of her daughter's relationship, the Colonel was livid once again. Elvis demanded Juanico call her mother and tell her to stay away from reporters. The incidents were telltale signs that when push came to shove, Elvis put the Colonel, his career, and even his fast-paced lifestyle first.

Like Dixie, June did not particularly care for the group of cousins and friends who toured with Elvis, mostly because he changed when he was around them. Also like Dixie, she did not fit into the show business side of his life, though the stakes were higher by the fall of 1956. By this time, Elvis's real-life girlfriends had to compete with Hollywood actors and actresses, slimy hangers-on, and a bicoastal schedule of appearances and movies. The continuing upward spiral of Elvis's career distracted him, and the phone calls to June became less and less frequent. When Elvis did not call her on Christmas Day, June learned it was because a Las Vegas showgirl was spending the holidays with him and his family. Brokenhearted, she began dating other boys. Shortly thereafter, she met someone who, she explained, "swept me off my feet," and she married him.

The next small-town girl with whom Elvis got involved was Anita Wood, who was from Jackson, Tennessee, and who had show business ambitions herself. A beauty-contest winner, she was also a local Memphis television personality and disc jockey. She and Elvis began dating in 1957 after his buddy George Klein arranged an introduction. Though Elvis was no longer a teenager in love, Anita was just 19 when they began seriously dating. Anita was often photographed saying goodbye to Elvis as he left for Hollywood, a new tour, a recording session, or eventually the army in March 1958.

Anita was there for Elvis when his mother died in August 1958, consoling him as best she could. A Memphis newspaper leaked that Anita and Elvis would marry before he left for his tour of army duty in Germany the following month, but Anita fended off the report as mere rumor. Though Anita wrote regularly to Elvis in Germany, he was reluctant to have her visit him there. Shortly after Elvis returned home to Memphis, he and Anita resumed a relationship, but his situation had changed. Just a few weeks before his army service was up, he had met 14-year-old Priscilla Beaulieu—the girl he would eventually mold into the woman of his dreams.

Anita wanted to get married and have a family, something she finally realized was never going to happen with Elvis Presley. In the summer of 1962, she broke off their relationship. Like Dixie Locke and June Juanico before her, Anita wisely gave up the most sought-after man in the world to pursue what she really wanted. Eventually, she married and had her own family.

Elvis with Anita Wood, a local TV personality whom he dated off and on from 1957 to the early 1960s.

MORE THAN JUST COSTARS

Early in his Hollywood career, Elvis developed a reputation for dating his costars while a movie was in production. Rumors about Elvis's crushes on actresses were always being repeated in fan magazines and elsewhere in the press. Much of what was said was obviously manufactured for its publicity value, but some of the rumors were undoubtedly true or came close to being true. To his credit, Colonel Parker kept information about Elvis's personal life to a minimum. He leaked just enough details about Elvis's Hollywood life to keep the news media away from Priscilla, who actually lived in Elvis's home, Graceland, although she and Elvis were not officially married.

Elvis kisses Ann-Margret, his love interest on- and off-screen during the shooting of Viva Las Vegas *(1964).*

Of all his relationships with his costars, Elvis's romance with Ann-Margret was probably the most serious. During the production of *Viva Las Vegas*, Elvis and the redheaded starlet set the publicity mill grinding out gossip when they began showing up together at restaurants and clubs around Las Vegas. They shared a mutual love for riding motorcycles and occasionally rode together, though they were warned to be careful because an accident involving either one of them would have delayed production on the movie.

The publicity surrounding the romance may have been a dream come true for the producers of *Viva Las Vegas*, but it must have been difficult for Priscilla. Secretly hidden from the public at Graceland, she undoubtedly saw the stories in Elvis's hometown newspaper, the *Memphis Press-Scimitar*, with headlines that blared "It Looks Like Romance for Elvis and Ann-Margret" and "Elvis Wins Love of Ann-Margret."

Although their romance did not work out, Elvis and Ann-Margret remained friends for the rest of his life. Elvis married Priscilla, and Ann-Margret married actor Roger Smith, but Elvis always sent Ann-Margret flowers in the shape of a guitar on the opening night of her Las Vegas engagements.

Elvis dated Tuesday Weld at the same time he was romancing Juliet Prowse, his costar from G.I. Blues.

Elvis also dated Tuesday Weld, his costar in *Wild in the Country*. Weld, who was barely 17 years old, was already a veteran of films and television as well as of the gossip columns. For good measure, Elvis also dated wardrobe girl Nancy Sharp about this time, whom he had met while filming *Flaming Star*. Other actresses whom Elvis dated during his career in Hollywood included Joan Blackman while working on *Kid Galahad*, Yvonne Craig while shooting *It Happened at the World's Fair*, Deborah Walley during the production of *Spinout*, and Mary Ann Mobley while working on *Girl Happy*.

A few actresses were notable for not dating Elvis during film production. Donna Douglas, costar of *Frankie and Johnny*, was a religious and spiritual person who impressed Elvis because she was so well read. He admired her intellect, and he was inspired by her example to read more, particularly books on religion and philosophy. Though Elvis tried desperately to get costar Shelley Fabares to go out with him during the production of *Girl Happy*, she was heavily involved with record producer Lou Adler and later married him. In lieu of a romantic relationship, Elvis and Fabares became friends. She costarred with him in two other movies, *Spinout* and *Clambake*, and Elvis later claimed that she was his favorite costar.

ELVIS AND THE BEAUTY QUEENS

Later in life, after he and Priscilla separated, Elvis's next major relationship was with beauty queen Linda Thompson, who was Miss Tennessee at the time. The 22-year-old beauty had been invited by a mutual acquaintance to the Memphian Theater for one of Elvis's after-hours movie viewings. She and Elvis hit it off, and the next night, they enjoyed their first official date. Thompson left for a three-week vacation with her family, and while she was gone, Elvis dated another Memphis beauty queen, Cybill Shepherd, who had just appeared in *The Heartbreak Kid*.

Elvis was more smitten with Thompson, however, and invited her to his Las Vegas engagement in the summer of 1972. He caught her at just the right time in her life. After her reign as Miss Tennessee, she did not know whether to return to college, move to New York to pursue modeling, or try her luck in Los Angeles. She was ready to experience more of the world but was undecided which direction to take.

The invitation to join Elvis's world made the decision for her. She adapted to his lifestyle and centered her life around him. But instead of expanding her world, living with Elvis actually shrank it. They lived in an isolated hothouse atmosphere that was dependent on either his schedule or his changing whims.

In 1974, their relationship began to deteriorate as Elvis's drug use increased and his physical and spiritual health declined. In 1975, Linda left for Los Angeles to pursue her acting career, though she still accompanied Elvis on some of his tours. The following year, she left him for good, realizing that she couldn't make him happy or make him change his destructive lifestyle.

Memphis-born Ginger Alden was Elvis's last serious relationship. Longtime friend George Klein introduced the singer to the woman who would be his next girlfriend. Klein brought Alden and her older sister, Terry, to meet Elvis, though Klein thought that the singer might prefer Terry. Like Linda Thompson and Cybill Shepherd, the Alden sisters were beauty queens. Terry was the reigning Miss Tennessee, and 20-year-old Ginger was Miss Mid-South. Ginger became an official part of the entourage when she joined Elvis on tour in November 1976.

Ginger does not fit into the Elvis Presley myth and legend as nicely as Priscilla, who is still described as his true love, or Linda, who was well liked for her loyalty. According to some in his inner circle, Elvis asked Ginger to marry him because he was worn out,

A Date With Elvis at the Memphian

During the 1960s, Elvis began renting theaters and amusement parks after hours so that he could relax with some of his favorite activities but still have privacy. One venue that he rented regularly was the Memphian Theater on Cooper Street. The owner of the Memphian opened the theater after hours especially for Elvis, and he and his buddy bodyguards attended special film showings beginning at midnight. The bodyguards were allowed to bring outsiders, and sometimes the outsiders were allowed to bring friends as well. It was a way for Elvis and his friends to experience one of the most traditional dating activities—going to the movies—without the intrusion of the public. Elvis took many of his girlfriends to these after-hours affairs, and he met some of them there, including Linda Thompson.

The restored Memphian is now included as part of several Elvis Presley tours.

depressed, and lost in a haze of drug-induced disillusionment. Jeweler Lowell Hays claimed that Elvis had a diamond ring made for her from his own TCB ring and proposed to her in January 1977. Whether he would have gone through with the marriage is still debated by those close to him. Alden might have been forgotten in the Elvis story if not for the fact that she discovered his body when he died on August 16, 1977.

PRISCILLA BEAULIEU PRESLEY

Elvis's fateful meeting with Priscilla occured while he was stationed in Germany during his stint in the Army. Much has been made of the fact that Priscilla was only 14 when the pair was introduced, but the young girl was mature for her age, and Elvis was mindful of the implications of the situation. Priscilla was photographed by the press at the airport when Elvis left the base in Germany to return to America, and some of those photos ended up in *Life* magazine. Beyond this, there was surprisingly little publicity about their relationship.

Elvis and Priscilla relax in Palm Springs after their wedding.

Priscilla visited Elvis at his home, Graceland, many times over the next couple of years, and Elvis began pressuring her parents to let her stay in Memphis. In 1962, he finally persuaded the Beaulieus to allow her to live with his father and stepmother, Vernon and Dee Presley, and attend school in Memphis. Gradually, Priscilla moved into Graceland while still underage. The press would have gone into a feeding frenzy if this information had leaked out, but while Priscilla was finishing high school, her private life remained private. More than likely, Colonel Tom Parker was responsible for keeping the news media at bay. He understood the press sharks and knew when and what to feed them. The dozens of stories about Elvis dating his leading ladies in Hollywood have become part of his image as a womanizer who chased the girls until they allowed him to catch them. Some of these stories were true, and some weren't, but they all created a smokescreen that protected Priscilla in Memphis.

On May 1, 1967, Elvis married Priscilla at the Aladdin Hotel in Las Vegas. The double-ring ceremony lasted only eight minutes and took place in the suite of one of the Colonel's associates. Only a few of Elvis's friends were allowed to witness the actual

Lisa Marie Presley

After her father's death in 1977, Elvis's only daughter was shielded from the public and the mainstream press by her mother, Priscilla Presley, who perhaps took a page out of Colonel Parker's book regarding the news media. As an adult, Lisa Marie appeared in the news upon occasion, but she never actively courted the press.

Her relationship with her father's fans was connected to her role in his estate, which includes Graceland. She was scheduled to inherit the estate when she turned 25 in 1993. Instead, she formed a new trust, the Elvis Presley Trust, and retained the original three executors, including her mother. Five years later, her mother handed the trust over to Lisa Marie.

In 2003, Lisa Marie surprised the music industry and Elvis's fans by launching a career as a rock 'n' roll singer. Her debut album was titled *To Whom It May Concern,* and it reached number five on the Billboard 200, an albums chart. She released her second album, *Now What,* in 2005, and it reached number nine on the Billboard 200. With her hard-rocking sound, she carved out her own niche in contemporary music—no small feat considering the act she had to follow.

Elvis and Lisa Marie, December 1970.

event, causing some dissension in the ranks of his buddy bodyguards. Afterward, there was a breakfast reception for 100 at the Aladdin, which was an event held primarily for the press. Elvis and Priscilla honeymooned in Palm Springs, California, and then split their time between Graceland and their new home in Beverly Hills.

On February 1, 1968, nine months to the day after Elvis and Priscilla were married, Lisa Marie Presley was born.

ARMY YEARS

Fans and critics alike wondered if Elvis's career was coming to an end when he began military service. Yet, it wasn't all worry and no play for US 53 310 761.

On the night of Sunday, March 23, 1958, Elvis was riding the crest of a wave of popularity: Chart-topping records, hit movies, soldout concerts, fan hysteria, and nearconstant controversy all helped him become the biggest star on the planet. Yet on that March night, at the pinnacle of his

Elvis takes a bus bound for Kennedy Veterans Hospital in Memphis, where he and 12 other Army recruits were examined and processed.

Anita Wood made frequent visits to Fort Hood, Texas, while Elvis was undergoing basic training.

success, with the world at his feet and an omnipresent support system of fans, relatives, and friends, it seemed as if he was giving it all away.

For more than a year the specter of military service hung over his head. When Uncle Sam came calling, Elvis passed his pre-induction physical and considered his options. Instead of taking the easy route chosen by so many celebrities in his position—entering Special Services to entertain the troops—he decided to show his allegiance to the Stars and Stripes by serving his time as a regular soldier. In the face of overexposure and negative publicity about his destabilizing influence on American youth, Elvis's refusal to accept special consideration was received by the public in an admirable light. Though he made the most of his last night as a civilian, he seemed understandably upset about leaving his friends and loved ones and giving up the good life. And, while making positive comments to press reporters, he was also said to be privately concerned that, after two years away, he'd never be able to pick up where he left off.

On the morning of March 24, accompanied by his parents, girlfriend Anita Wood, and various friends, Elvis reported to the draft board in the M&M Building on South Main Street in Memphis, and was soon traveling on a bus toward the Kennedy Veterans Hospital, where he and twelve other recruits were examined and processed. Pronounced fit, Private Elvis Presley US 53 310 761 bid farewell to his distraught mother, weeping father, and Anita, and boarded yet another bus, this one bound for Fort Chaffee, Arkansas. Several hundred fans were in tow, as well as a posse of reporters and photographers intent on recording his every word and action, from folding his civilian clothes to making his army bed.

The next day, after undergoing further

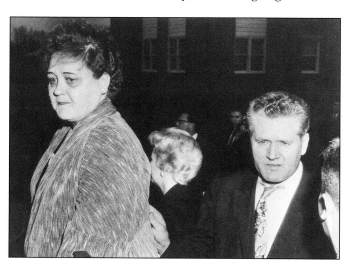

Vernon and Gladys Presley share a sad moment after watching their son board a bus bound for Fort Chaffee, Arkansas.

This is one of the last photos of Elvis with his mother. Gladys became ill while living off-base with Elvis in Fort Hood, returned to Memphis with acute hepatitis, and died there on August 14, 1958.

cameras, Elvis good-naturedly submitted himself to a standard-issue GI cut . . . . and promptly forgot to hand over the 65¢ fee out of the generous $7 partial pay that he'd been given a short time earlier. While a porter used a broom to sweep up the famous locks and discarded fragments of sideburn, the barber reminded Elvis that he owed some money.

Subsequently issued his U.S. Army uniform, Private Presley was assigned to the 2nd Armored Division at Fort Hood, Texas, for basic training and advanced tank instruction. Fans and members of the media followed him all the way there before Elvis's military superiors declared him off limits to reporters and photographers following his first 24 hours at Fort Hood. Once the immediate attention subsided, Elvis adapted to life with his fellow recruits, though he seemed desperately homesick at times. He phoned Gladys at least once a day, and many times both of them were in tears, with Gladys begging him to take proper care of himself and Elvis trying to reassure his worried mother. While some of the soldiers gave him a hard time about his

processing procedures, the King of Rock 'n' Roll was given the most famous haircut since Samson was tricked by Delilah. Before popping flashbulbs and whirring news

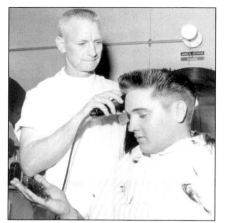

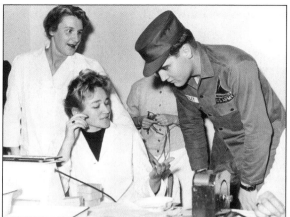

Top left: In front of the world's cameras, Elvis says good-bye to his famous locks and long sideburns.

Top right: The King chats with a young nurse before donating blood for the German Red Cross in January 1959. He was one of 200 American soldiers giving blood that day at the Friedberg dispensary.

Bottom left: Sporting a standard-issue GI haircut and white T-shirt, the singing soldier gets a shot from a smiling Army doctor during his pre-induction physical.

Above: On the morning of March 24, 1958, Elvis is sworn into the U.S. Army by an officer at the M&M Building on South Main Street in Memphis.

A few months after joining the 1st Medium Tank Battalion, 32nd Armor, 3rd Armored Division, Elvis was promoted to Private First Class for his endeavors in field exercises.

celebrity status, Elvis soon became friends with others such as Privates Rex Mansfield and William Norvell, as well as Sergeant Bill Norwood, who, after suggesting that Anita Wood should make a visit, made his own home available to her. Consequently, by the time Elvis completed basic training at the end of May, the teen idol had begun to settle in. He earned his marksman's medal with a carbine and was classified as a sharpshooter with a pistol. Elvis had always loved guns, so it made perfect sense that he would excel in these exercises.

On leave for two weeks at the start of June 1958, Elvis spent time with family and friends. He also recorded several new tracks in Nashville to help satisfy RCA's need for new material while he was out of commission. Then he returned to Fort Hood, and after receiving the standard soldier's permission to live off base with his "dependents," he obtained a three-bedroom

A smiling Elvis is captured by news cameras while on night maneuvers at the Grafenwohr exercise camp in December 1958. A week later he spent part of Christmas Eve helping to decorate the company's Christmas tree.

advanced tank training during the week. Friends from all over would drop by, and Gladys would prepare food for everyone. All in all it was a pretty cozy setup until Gladys's health declined, and she and Vernon had to return to Memphis at the start of August.

Ever since her son's induction, Gladys had been anxious about his well-being and distraught at the thought of his absence for an extended period of time. Now extremely sick and unable to eat, Gladys was admitted to Methodist Hospital on August 9 with acute hepatitis. Having completed his advanced tank training, Elvis was about to commence his basic unit training, but it quickly became clear that his mother's condition was serious. On August 12 the Army granted him emergency leave. Elvis headed straight for the hospital, and when his mother saw him she appeared to rally. However, during the early hours of Thursday, August 14, 1958, with Vernon by her side while Elvis was at home, Gladys Love Presley succumbed to a

trailer home and moved there with his parents, grandmother Minnie Mae, and friend Lamar Fike. When the trailer became a little too cramped, following the arrival of cousins Gene and Junior Smith, he simply rented a house where he could stay with his family on the weekends while undergoing

All Aboard!

Fans and media representatives turned out in force when Elvis was due to board ship for his military trip to Europe. So, with Colonel Parker orchestrating the proceedings, and to the strains of an Army band playing "Tutti Frutti," Elvis put on his best smile for the cameras as he walked up the gangplank of the U.S.S. *General Randall* . . . . and walked, and walked, and walked. In total, he went through the boarding routine eight times until everyone was satisfied, and then soon afterward, while the band played a medley of his hits, the ship set sail and Elvis left the United States for the first and, as things would turn out, only time.

massive heart attack. She was just 46. It was a blow from which Elvis would never seem to fully recover.

Elvis broke down several times in the days leading up to his mother's funeral. He sobbed hysterically while Gladys's favorite gospel group, the Blackwood Brothers, performed at the service in the Memphis Funeral Home, and he was equally inconsolable at her Forest Hill Cemetery grave site, crying out, "Oh God, everything I have is gone."

The mourning continued through the next few days as Elvis was granted extended leave. Evidently his fans were grieving too—they sent him more than 100,000 cards and letters, around 500 telegrams, and more than 200 floral arrangements to express their sympathy for his loss. Still, even though it would never be the same, life had to carry on. Elvis returned to Fort Hood on August 24, and within a month he shipped out to join the 1st Medium Tank Battalion, 32nd Armor, 3rd Armored Division in what was

146

then known as West Germany. Along the way, Colonel Tom Parker organized a press conference when Elvis's troop train arrived in Brooklyn, New York, at which he answered questions about his army duty, his music, and his mom. He offered a heartfelt account of his continued mourning to the assembled reporters:

> Everyone loses their mother, but I was an only child, and Mother was always right with me all my life. And it wasn't only like losing a mother, it was like losing a friend, a companion, someone to talk to. I could wake her up any hour of the night if I was worried or troubled about something . . . . she'd get up and try to help me.

During the transatlantic trip aboard the U.S.S. *General Randall*, Elvis bonded with a fellow singer named Charlie Hodge, whom he'd met on the troop train to Brooklyn, and together they took charge of a talent show. But without his mother to see or talk to ever again, Elvis seemed lonely and adrift.

In West Germany, there was another press conference and

further meet-and-greets during the first few days. Vernon and his mother, Minnie Mae—whom Elvis had affectionately called "Dodger" ever since she had ducked

Fatigued in his fatigues: Elvis takes time out to read some fan mail.

Change of Address

Elvis, Vernon, Minnie Mae, Red West, Lamar Fike, and Elisabeth Stefaniak occupied the top floor of the refined Hotel Grunewald in Bad Nauheim, but they quickly fell out of favor with the management and other guests thanks to the unruly behavior of the King and his courtiers. Vernon, Minnie Mae, and Elisabeth weren't the problem; it was the other three, constantly roughhousing with one another to the point where nobody could get any peace and quiet. One night at the end of January 1959 their antics went too far. Elvis, chased by Red down a hallway, locked himself in his bedroom, and Red tried to smoke him out by setting fire to a piece of paper and sliding it under his door. Before they knew it, the flames were out of control. When the manager, Herr Schmidt, learned about the incident, Elvis and company were asked to leave the hotel. The group soon found a rental house at 14

Goethestrasse (pictured), where they lived for the duration of Elvis's tour of duty.

away from a ball he had thrown at her as a child—set up residence with Elvis and his friends Red West and Lamar Fike in a couple of hotels: one in Bad Homburg, near Frankfurt; the other in Bad Nauheim, about 20 minutes from the base. Elvis would rise every morning at 5:30, eat the

Elvis signs autographs for fans while on leave in Paris. He visited the French capital on two occasions during his time in the Army.

breakfast Dodger had prepared for him, and leave for base by 6:30 in a black Mercedes taxi, before returning for lunch and dinner. The only exception was Friday, when Elvis and his fellow soldiers had to stay late into the evening, cleaning the toilets and their barracks for weekly inspection the following morning. It had been a long time since the King was obliged to do any such chores, yet he mucked in with the other soldiers and did his best to be perceived—during the day, at least—as just a regular guy.

Some evenings, Elvis and his friends surreptitiously went to the movies—sneaking into theaters after the lights went down and leaving just before the final credits to avoid being noticed—and even to a couple of Bill Haley concerts. Elvis also dated a few girls while keeping in regular phone contact with Anita Wood back in America. Through November and much of December, Private Presley went on maneuvers at Grafenwohr and was promoted to Private First Class for his endeavors in field exercises. It was reportedly around this time that one of the sergeants introduced him to amphetamines as a means of staying alert and awake during the long hours of training. For Elvis, taking amphetamines would quickly become a regular habit.

Although he returned to Bad Nauheim to spend most of the holiday season with family and friends, he also spent part of

Christmas Eve helping to decorate the company's Christmas tree. Then, at the start of January 1959, one of the girls whom Elvis had briefly dated, 19-year-old Elisabeth Stefaniak, moved into the Hotel Grunewald with him and his inner circle, having accepted an invitation to work as his secretary. It was particularly handy that, courtesy of her German mother and American stepfather, Elisabeth was bilingual. So, installing herself in a corner room at the hotel, she answered his fan mail and became romantically involved with him despite the understanding that he would continue to see other girls.

In early February, the Presley clan relocated to a three-story, five-bedroom house at Goethestrasse 14, which afforded everyone more space and privacy than the nearby Hotel Grunewald. For the exorbitant rent of $800 a month, it also provided them with a landlady named Frau Pieper who doubled as their housekeeper. At last, Elvis was living in a home where he could relax away from prying eyes, listen to records, entertain friends, and sit at a piano to play and sing his favorite songs. He came home every day for lunch, and each evening he would spend time signing autographs for fans who waited patiently in front of the house. On Sundays he and some friends would play touch football just down the street.

Early in 1959, accompanied by friends Red West and Lamar Fike, Elvis used a three-day pass to visit Munich and call unannounced on Vera Tschechowa, an 18-year-old actress whom he'd met a few months earlier. Together, they visited the Moulin Rouge nightclub. As usual, the press was on hand to photograph Elvis with his

A somber young Priscilla bids Elvis farewell at the Rhein-Main air base in Germany.

Fans peer through the window as Elvis and Priscilla share a moment alone on the way to the airport for his return to the United States.

"latest flame." In this case they also took numerous shots of him posing with the club's showgirls, but all it really amounted to was a footloose and fancy-free young man having some fun. Enough fun, in fact, for him to pay a return visit to Munich's Moulin Rouge nightclub in mid-June before continuing his two-week furlough by traveling to Paris and dropping in on the original Moulin Rouge.

By June, Red West had returned to the United States, so Elvis was accompanied by Lamar Fike as well as his two army buddies Charlie Hodge and Rex Mansfield when visiting Parisian nightspots including the Lido, the Folies Bergère, and a club called Le Bantu that didn't even open until 4:00 A.M. All in all, the Paris stopover was reported to have been a live-by-night, sleep-by-day

Elvis meets the press on March 3, 1960, just two days before his discharge from the U.S. Army. He answered questions on several topics, including his relationship with 14-year old Priscilla Beaulieu.

a sensuous mouth and sultry blue eyes, she was wearing a navy and white sailor dress with white socks and shoes; he, a bright red sweater and tan slacks. Brenda Lee's "Sweet Nothin's" was spinning on the record player.

Priscilla, as can be expected, seemed in awe of the superstar, while Elvis was said to be instantly infatuated with the beautiful stepdaughter of Air Force Captain Joseph Beaulieu. Captain Beaulieu had been transferred to Wiesbaden, a 45-minute drive from Bad Nauheim, just a month earlier, and Priscilla had been invited to visit Elvis at his home by mutual acquaintance Currie Grant, a U.S. Airman and assistant manager at Wiesbaden air force venue the Eagle Club.

Elvis spent the rest of that Sunday evening talking to Priscilla and, amid a room full of friends, even sang to her. It wasn't long before he asked Currie Grant to invite her back.

Soon Elvis and Priscilla began dating, and after Elvis met Priscilla's parents and convinced them that his intentions were honorable, they saw each other frequently during his last few months in West Germany. Because of Elvis's inability to go

adventure. Elvis returned to the French capital for one last adventure in January 1960, although by then a new girl was occupying his thoughts.

Fourteen-year-old Priscilla Beaulieu had only recently been voted "Queen of Del Valley Junior High" by her classmates in Austin, Texas, when 24-year-old Elvis Presley first met her on the evening of Sunday, September 13, 1959. Brunette, with out in public unrecognized (and without creating a mob scene), most of his dates with Priscilla consisted of her visits to his house, where they were surrounded by Elvis's family members and friends. Although a relationship with someone so young could have had a ruinous effect on Elvis's image, there was surprisingly little publicity about his interest in Priscilla.

Elvis was promoted to sergeant on January 20, 1960, received his stripes on February 11, and was scheduled to be discharged from the Army in early March. Accordingly, he began preparing for the resumption of his life at Graceland and his career in Nashville and Hollywood, sending old girlfriend Anita Wood a French poodle for Christmas and calling her more frequently as his return to America drew closer.

Regardless, word of his relationship with Priscilla did reach the media, and on March 2, the day of his departure from West Germany, press photographers and news cameras captured her somber face as she waved good-bye to her love at the Rhein-Main airbase. The photos ended up in *Life* magazine, and Priscilla was labeled "the girl he left behind." Which she was . . . . for the time being.

Discharged on Saturday, March 5, after disembarking in Fort Dix, New Jersey, Elvis finally arrived back in Memphis two days later amid a snowstorm and much hoopla. That afternoon, sitting in his father's office behind the main house at Graceland, he gave a press conference, during which he acknowledged—yet tried to play down—his relationship with Priscilla Beaulieu, focusing instead on how happy he was to be back home. "I just can't get it in my mind that I'm here," he told the media.

Elvis wasn't the only Presley to find a new love in Germany. His father, Vernon, met Dee Stanley while the Presley family was living in Bad Nauheim. At the time they met, Dee was in the process of divorcing her military husband. Dee returned to America with Vernon after Elvis's discharge, and the two were married in Huntsville, Alabama, in July 1960. Elvis did not attend his father's wedding, which led to speculation that the marriage caused friction between the two men. (Elvis not only gained a stepmother, but he got three stepbrothers as well.)

As time would tell, Elvis was a changed man when he emerged from the Army. Critics speculated that the damage done to his career during his two years in the Army could be irreparable. Instead, Elvis surprised everyone by trading in the frenzied trappings of his rock 'n' roll youth for a more mature image built on the good publicity from his tour of duty. The success of his movies and pop music albums was a testament to the wide appeal of his new, more mellow style.

Sergeant Presley was greeted by Frank Sinatra's 19-year-old daughter, Nancy, after disembarking in Fort Dix, New Jersey, just prior to his discharge from the Army.

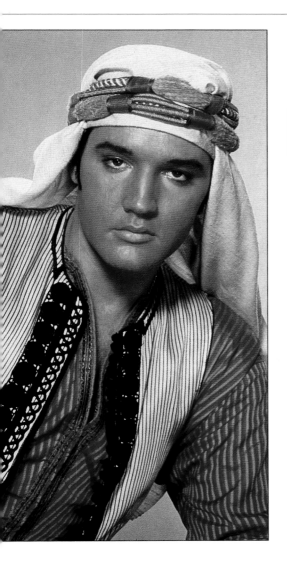

ELVIS IN FILM

"A **Presley picture** is the only **sure thing** in Hollywood."

—PRODUCER HAL WALLIS

Nothing incites more disagreement among biographers, fans, and music critics than Elvis Presley's career as a **leading man** in Hollywood movies. Often blamed for a perceived decline in his music, the movies are generally disliked and harshly criticized by biographers and rock 'n' roll fans. Elvis himself disliked the musical comedies he made, and was disappointed that he was unable to stretch his acting abilities in other genres.

However, an updated consideration of his films results in an alternative view. While most of Elvis's musicals are not classics, he certainly appeared in more well-crafted films than most pop performers of the period. Furthermore, none of his movies lost money for the studios that financed them, and, in retrospect, they offer wholesome entertainment that is in keeping with the traditional musical. Some of the songs and production numbers were poorly written and conceived, but some of his movie tunes became pop classics, with several having enjoyed a revival. Viewed today, many of the production numbers have a campy appeal that offers insight into the fads and trends of another era.

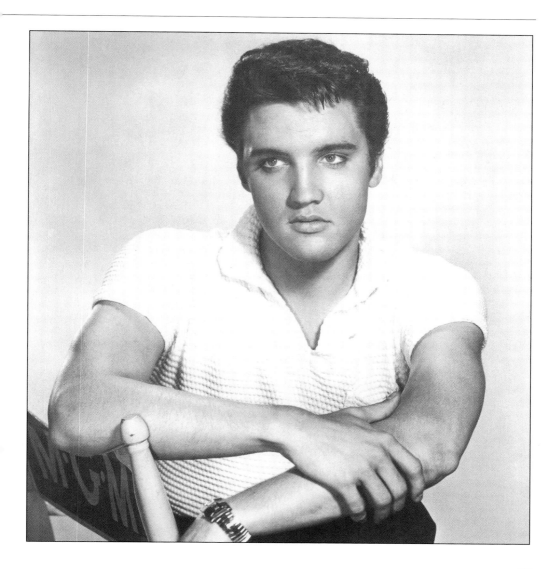

ELVIS'S FIRST *Film*

Love Me Tender

In this drama set immediately after the Civil War, Elvis costars as Clint, the youngest son in the Reno family. This was the only time in his acting career that Elvis played a secondary role.

Elvis's first experience as a Hollywood actor was closely followed in the entertainment press from the day he was assigned a role in *Love Me Tender* until the day the film was released. This close scrutiny affected the outcome of the film in several ways. Originally called *The Reno Brothers*, this western drama was retitled after a number of articles announced that advance sales for "Love Me Tender"—one of the songs recorded for the film—had surpassed a million copies. It was the first time that advance sales for a single release had ever exceeded the million mark, and the producers adroitly capitalized on this publicity by changing the film's title.

The enormous amount of press coverage also affected the film's conclusion. During production, fanzines leaked that Elvis's character was supposed to die near the end of the film. As originally shot, the final scene features Mother Reno solemnly ringing the dinner bell as her three remaining sons toil in the fields. Pain and loss are registered on the faces of Mother Reno and Cathy, who mourn the death of Clint. Elvis's legion of fans was disturbed by the news that their idol was to be killed off in his first film. In an attempt to counter an "adverse public reaction," 20th Century-Fox shot an alternative ending in which Clint is spared. This second ending was rejected, and a compromise ending was

used instead. Clint is killed as called for in the original script, but the final shot superimposed a ghostly close-up of Elvis as Clint crooning "Love Me Tender" as his family slowly walks away from his grave. The fans were then left with a final image of Elvis doing what he was famous for—singing.

ELVIS'S FIRST *Line*

Movie Dialogue

Clint (Elvis):
Whoa! Brett, Vance
. . . . They told us
you were dead!

"That boy could **charm the birds from the trees.** He was so eager and humble, we went out of our way to help him."

—RICHARD EGAN, WHO PLAYED OLDER BROTHER VANCE RENO IN *LOVE ME TENDER*

PANNED IN THE PRESS

Some of the reviews for Elvis's performance in *Love Me Tender* were brutal, though many critics seemed prejudiced by the negative press over his controversial performing style as a singer.

"Is it a sausage? It is certainly smooth and damp-looking. Is it a Walt Disney goldfish? It has the same sort of big, soft, beautiful eyes and long, curly lashes . . . . **Is it a corpse?** The face just hangs there, limp and white with its little drop-seat mouth, rather like Lord Byron in the wax museum."

—*TIME*

"*Love Me Tender* will have no place in motion picture history, but it may very well have a place in the history of American morals and mores, for Presley is a pied piper who could lead his followers to an end more socially deleterious than their permanent disappearance in a cave."

—HENRY HART, *FILMS IN REVIEW*

"....in a magnificent death scene ....oddly, he reminds one of Liberace."

—HOLLIS ALPERT, *THE SATURDAY REVIEW*

"Appraising Presley **as an actor, he ain't.** Not that it makes much difference. The presence of Presley apparently is enough to satisfy the juve [juvenile] set."

—*VARIETY*

Loving You

Elvis Presley was not simply the star of *Loving You*; in a sense, he was also the subject. The film served as a vehicle built around Elvis's image and was designed to showcase his rock 'n' roll music and explosive performing style. The storyline, costuming, and music incorporated specific characteristics strongly associated with the real-life Elvis Presley and then manipulated them to suit specific ends.

The ultimate effect was a reshaping of Elvis's rebel image into one more recognizable and therefore more acceptable to mainstream audiences.

Some of Elvis's family and friends appear in *Loving You* in cameos and bit parts. His parents, Gladys and Vernon, appear as members of the audience in the final production number. Real-life band members Scotty Moore, Bill Black, and D. J. Fontana have bit parts as Elvis's bandmates.

The "Teddy Bear" Costume

Elvis's purported fondness for teddy bears was likely just a publicity stunt manufactured by the Colonel in the 1950s. One offshoot of the story holds that Kal Mann and Bernie Lowe composed the song "Teddy Bear" for Elvis supposedly as a response to the rumors. Elvis performed the song in his second film, *Loving You*, which was shot in glorious Technicolor. The cinematography, with its rich, saturated colors, proved the perfect vehicle to exploit the film's 1950s-style costumes. For the "Teddy Bear" number, Elvis wore a silky, maroon and white, western-style outfit. The engaging love song combined with the endearing ensemble served to soften Elvis's rebellious persona. Aside from being a fan favorite, the costume gained attention when it was discussed on *You Bet Your Life*, a television game show hosted by Groucho Marx. The president of the San Diego Elvis Presley Fan Club, who had purchased the costume, appeared on the show, and Groucho teased her about her passion for Elvis and her unusual acquisition.

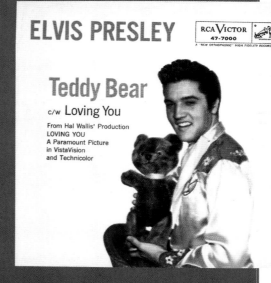

ELVIS'S FIRST *Kiss*

Elvis received his **first passionate on-screen kiss** in his second feature, *Loving You.* Actress Jana Lund bestowed the legendary kiss, which was the one act that made her minor screen career memorable. Other films she appeared in included the teen flicks *Don't Knock the Rock, High School Hellcats,* and *Hot Car Girl.* Her last screen appearance was in *Married Too Young* in 1962.

SpotLight On

Jailhouse Rock

King Creole boasts a powerful cast and a skilled director, and *Blue Hawaii* features slick production values, but the gritty, low-budget *Jailhouse Rock* remains Elvis Presley's best film. Elvis the rock 'n' roll rebel liberated a generation from the values, tastes, and ideals of their parents, and *Jailhouse Rock* is the only Presley film that speaks directly to the feral, sensual, and unruly nature of rock 'n' roll music.

The heart of *Jailhouse Rock* is the character of Vince Everett, who swaggers and prowls through the film with attitude and magnetism. Despite his Hollywood-style conversion in the final moments, it is Vince's impudence and haughty defiance that stay with the viewer long after the final fadeout. The character embodies the rebellious spirit of rock 'n' roll, in much the same way that Elvis did in his career. This close identification between real-life performer and fictional character is not a detriment; indeed, it is the film's strength.

FAVORITE DIALOGUE FROM ELVIS FLICKS

Peggy: How dare you think that cheap tactics would work with me?

Vince (Elvis): Them ain't tactics honey. That's just the beast in me!

—*JAILHOUSE ROCK*

Jailhouse Rock's most famous production number was

choreographed by Elvis himself.

Myth vs. Fact

The scene in which the prison barber shaves off Elvis's infamous ducktail made fans weep and parents cheer. Over the years, much speculation existed as to whether it was Elvis's **real hair** that was cut **or a wig.** A glance at the production schedule as reprinted in Jim Hannaford's *Inside Jailhouse Rock* reveals the truth: Two wigs were used to represent Elvis's atrocious prison 'do. The schedule indicates that Elvis had to film three scenes in one week—one with the butch haircut, one with the hair partially grown back, and one with his regular style. Obviously, his real hair could not have grown back in that short span of time. In later years, makeup artist William Tuttle revealed that a series of plaster casts of Elvis's head allowed them to make wigs that fit so well that they were nearly impossible to detect.

Penned by the legendary Jerry Leiber and Mike Stoller, **"Jailhouse Rock"** became another big hit for Elvis. It entered the British charts at number one, making it the first single ever to do so. The rock 'n' roll songwriting duo was commissioned to write most of the songs from the movie *Jailhouse Rock*, though they were less than enthusiastic about the assignment.

During the April 1957 recording session for "Jailhouse Rock," Leiber and Stoller quickly changed their minds about Elvis when they realized he knew his music and that he was a workhorse in the studio. The pair took over the recording sessions, serving as unofficial producers of "Jailhouse Rock," "Treat Me Nice," "(You're So Square) Baby, I Don't Care," and other tunes. Their collaboration with Elvis and his musicians on "Jailhouse Rock" resulted in the singer's hardest-rocking movie song. As D. J. Fontana once noted about his drum playing on the record, "I tried to think of someone on a chain gang smashing rocks."

GREAT MOVIE TUNES

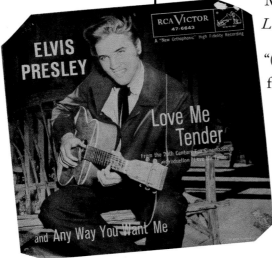

"Love Me Tender" from
Love Me Tender

"Teddy Bear" from *Loving You*

"Mean Woman Blues" from
Loving You

"(You're So Square) Baby, I Don't Care"
from *Jailhouse Rock*

"Treat Me Nice" from

Jailhouse Rock

"Trouble" from *King Creole*

"New Orleans" from *King Creole*

"Hard Headed Woman"
from *King Creole*

"G.I. Blues" from *G.I. Blues*

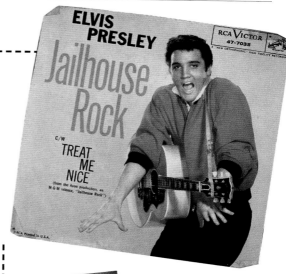

HAL B. WALLIS

Hal Wallis, a respected veteran of the film industry, worked in Hollywood from the silent era through the 1970s. He began as a publicity representative for Warner Brothers, working his way up to executive producer in charge of production by 1933. There he produced several classics, including *Little Caesar*, *Sergeant York*, and *The Maltese Falcon*. In 1944, he became an independent producer, releasing his films through Paramount and later Universal. As an independent, Wallis had a reputation for fostering new talent and was dubbed "the Discoverer." Among those whose screen careers he helped were Kirk Douglas, the team of Dean Martin and Jerry Lewis, Shirley MacLaine, and Elvis Presley.

Of the nine films that Wallis produced starring Elvis, Wallis's personal favorite was *King Creole*. He once said that one of the biggest regrets in his career was that he was not able to follow through on his idea for a western starring John Wayne as an older gunfighter with Elvis as his protégé. Wallis died in 1986.

"When I ran the test, I felt the same thrill I experienced when I first saw Errol Flynn on the screen. **Elvis,** in a very different, modern way, had exactly the same **power, virility, and sexual drive.** The camera caressed him."

—Hal Wallis, *Starmaker,* on Elvis's screen test

King Creole *was considered a major Hollywood production. Director Michael Curtiz (far left) and producer Hal Wallis confer* *with Elvis behind the scenes.*

"Anybody who will **pay my boy a million dollars** can make any kind of [motion] picture they want."

—Colonel Tom Parker, 1960s

King Creole

A musical drama with a cast of Hollywood's most respected character actors, *King Creole* was directed by veteran Michael Curtiz and produced by Hal Wallis for Paramount Pictures. Though not a classic, it is a well-crafted example of a typical Hollywood film from the era when the studio system still dominated the industry. In this production, which was less of a vehicle designed around Elvis than the majority of his movies were, the young actor held his own with a cast of talented professionals. *King Creole* now stands as a testament to Elvis's acting potential, which was never fully realized in the succession of teen musicals he made in the 1960s.

Elvis worked with a number of talented character actors and veteran movie stars throughout his career, but he rarely had a supporting cast of the caliber of *King Creole*. Some of the cast members were at the peak of their careers; some were established supporting players who had been a part of Hollywood for several years; some were relative unknowns at the start of lucrative careers. Elvis's stellar costars on this film included Carolyn Jones, Walter Matthau, Dolores Hart, Dean Jagger, and Vic Morrow.

Lobby card for King Creole

"He was an instinctive actor .... He was quite bright
.... **He was not a punk.** He was very elegant,
sedate, and refined, and sophisticated."

—WALTER MATTHAU,
ON COSTARRING WITH ELVIS IN *KING CREOLE*,
1987 INTERVIEW

"He's the **best-mannered star** in Hollywood, and he's improved as a performer and has determination to be a fine actor. [Elvis] was smart enough to simmer down that torrid act of his."

—HEDDA HOPPER, EARLY 1960S

Elvis and Nancy Sinatra

On his return from the army in 1960, Elvis was scheduled to appear on *Welcome Home, Elvis*, a television special hosted by Frank Sinatra. Frank sent his daughter Nancy to the airport as Elvis's official greeter. The pair struck up a friendship that lasted for years and provided sparkling chemistry in *Speedway*. Her version of "Your Groovy Self" was included on the soundtrack album, marking the only time another artist sang a solo on a regular RCA Elvis album. In the mid–1960s, Nancy recorded four hit duets with singer- songwriter Lee Hazlewood, who also wrote her best-known hit, "These Boots Are Made for Walking." Nancy earned her third gold record for a duet she sang with her father, "Something Stupid." She also spent a large part of the 1960s cavorting through teen musicals such as *Get Yourself a College Girl* (1964) and *The Ghost in the Invisible Bikini* (1966). During the mid–1990s, Nancy rode the crest of a nostalgia wave, singing her 1960s hits to a new generation and appearing in *Playboy* magazine.

"He is no longer the sneering, hip-twitching symbol of the untamed beast that resides in 17-year-old breasts. He has come back from the Army **easygoing, unassuming. . . ."**

—*LIFE*, OCTOBER 10, 1960

It was shortly after Elvis's discharge from the army that the entertainment press discovered that he was accompanied by an entourage of about 20 friends and associates wherever he traveled. This detail provided the origin of the

"Memphis Mafia"

(or the "Tennessee Mafia") term, just as they had called Frank Sinatra's gang of celebrity friends the "Rat Pack." However, the differences between the Rat Pack and the Memphis Mafia became apparent as Elvis's career continued, and the press never quite seemed to grasp the gang's relationship to Elvis.

Most of the members of the Memphis Mafia were hometown boys from Memphis, family members, or friends Elvis had met in the army. Many of them actually lived with Elvis. They accompanied Elvis to the set, drove him to and from the studio, and worked as bodyguards to keep fans and the press away. The closeness of this group of friends and employees made Elvis feel at home in Hollywood or on the road, but it also isolated him from industry insiders and fellow entertainers who could have been a positive influence on him.

Elvis was infatuated with law enforcement most of his life. Here, Elvis and his entourage show off honorary deputy badges from Shelby County, Tennessee.

SPOTLIGHT ON

G.I. Blues

In May 1960, Elvis had returned to Hollywood to begin shooting *G.I. Blues*. The movie's storyline is about a singer serving in the U.S. army in Germany. Producer Hal Wallis freely borrowed details from Elvis's own life to flesh out the movie script just as he had done in the two previous films he worked on with Elvis. In *G.I. Blues,* Elvis's character is not only stationed abroad in Germany, he's also a member of a tank division just as Elvis had been.

Like the movies Elvis had made before going into the army, *G.I. Blues* is based on the events of his own life, but it is a musical comedy instead of a musical drama. *G.I. Blues* was aimed at a family audience, and Elvis's controversial performing style was toned down. Even though most of the songs are fast-paced, they don't have the same hard-driving sound, sexual connotation, or emotional delivery of Elvis's prior soundtrack recordings. Elvis's screen image was deliberately softened for

G.I. Blues. In one scene, he sings a Bavarian-sounding folk tune during a children's puppet show, while in another he baby-sits an adorable infant. The movie's ads perfectly sum up these changes: "See and Hear the New Elvis: The Idol of Teenagers Is the Idol of the Family."

G.I. Blues was enormously successful, ranking fourteenth in box-office receipts for 1960. Movie critics applauded the new Elvis. They approved of his new image and predicted he would find plenty of new fans among older women. Elvis didn't share the critics' enthusiasm for *G.I. Blues*. He felt that there were too many musical numbers and believed some of them made no sense within the context of the plot. He was concerned that the quality of many of these songs was not as good as the music from his earlier movies.

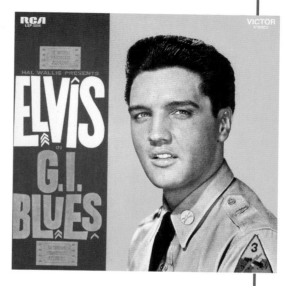

FAVORITE DIALOGUE FROM ELVIS FLICKS

Maile (soaking wet):
I bought this dress to welcome you home. It's the first time I've worn it.

Chad (Elvis): You know something? On you, wet is my favorite color.

—*BLUE HAWAII*

Much of *Blue Hawaii* was filmed on location in America's 50th state, which had only joined the union in 1959. Such beautiful Hawaiian locations as Waikiki Beach, Ala Moana Park, Lydgate Park, and the Coco Palms Resort Hotel were used in the film.

SPOTLIGHT ON

Blue Hawaii

"Exciting romance . . . . Dances . . . . Music in the World's Lushest Paradise of Song!" "Elvis Presley Guides You Through a Paradise of Song!" So blared the promotion for *Blue Hawaii*, Elvis's most financially successful film. Its lush location footage, large selection of songs, and colorful supporting cast accounted for its popularity, success, and good reputation, and that success and popularity determined the course of Elvis's movie career thereafter. With *Blue Hawaii*, a formula was established

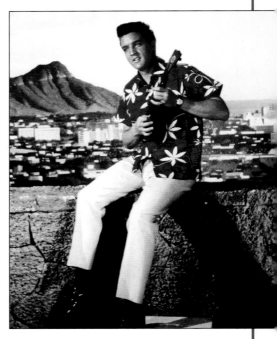

Elvis plays a singing tour guide in Blue Hawaii.

Elvis and Joan Blackman marry in a Hawaiian wedding ceremony in the beautiful final sequence of Blue Hawaii.

for Presley vehicles that was followed almost exclusively for the rest of his career. Exotic locales and vacation settings—and the romance and escape that went with them—became such well-known elements in certain Elvis movies that he disparagingly dubbed them the "Presley travelogues."

"Can't Help Falling in Love"

Written specifically for *Blue Hawaii* by George Weiss, Hugo Peretti, and Luigi Creatore, "Can't Help Falling in Love" is remembered as the ballad with which Elvis closed his concerts during the 1970s. In the film, Elvis's character sings it to his girlfriend's grandmother for her birthday, but that context has long since been forgotten. Because Elvis sang it so many times in concert, it is more fitting to suggest that the song belongs to the fans. It speaks to the way the fans felt about Elvis, and it was his love song to them.

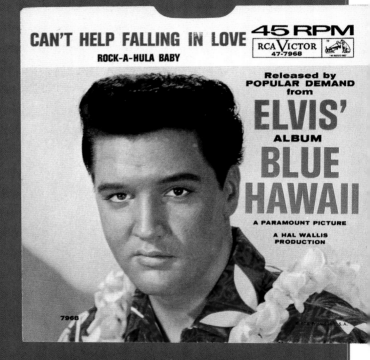

Record collectors should note that the movie version of "Can't falling in Love" was not the one released as a single or on the album. Two takes of the movie version were recorded along with one take of the single release. The movie version of "Can't Help Falling in Love" was not released until after Elvis's death.

In his musical comedies, Elvis often broke into song at any time, a characteristic he hated about his films. Here, he sings "Island of Love (Kauai)" to a tour group.

WHAT'S IN A NAME?

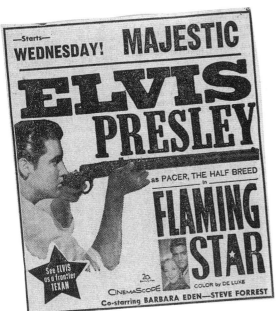

the originals. *Flaming Star* was at various times *Flaming Lance, Flaming Heart,* and *Black Star. In My Harem* became *Harem Holiday,* which turned into *Harem Scarum* and then finally *Harum Scarum,* with that all-important misspelling so that the first word could match the second. The memorable *Kiss My Firm But Pliant Lips* was changed to the forgettable *Live a Little, Love a Little. A Girl in Every Port* became *Welcome Aboard,* which became *Gumbo Ya-Ya,* which then became

Live a Little, Love a Little

Hollywood films commonly change their titles during production, but Elvis's musical comedies were notorious for doing this, often at the very last minute. Sometimes the change represented an improvement, as when *Hawaii Beach Boy* was given the much more romantic title *Blue Hawaii.* Usually, however, the final titles were little better than

Girls! Girls! Girls! Perhaps the worst series of titles belonged to *Spinout* because they were mostly meaningless clichés. Those considered included *Jim Dandy, After Midnight, Always at Midnight, Never Say No,* and *Never Say Yes.* To complicate matters, its British release title was *California Holiday.*

Spinout

FAVORITE DIALOGUE FROM ELVIS FLICKS

Bernice: I'll bet you're a marvelous lover.

Greg (Elvis): I'm representing the United States in the Olympics.

—*Live a Little, Love a Little*

Myth vs. FACT

Contrary to popular belief, Elvis appeared in more than just teen musicals during the 1960s. He starred in the western *Flaming Star,* the dramas *Wild in the Country* and *Kid Galahad,* and the satire *Follow That Dream.* These films are often pushed aside by biographers who want to paint the 1960s as a decline in Elvis's career or music historians and critics who blame the films for "taming" Elvis. Elvis's image did change after he returned from the army, and his music evolved into a mainstream pop style, but the changes were in keeping with the styles and trends of the early 1960s.

Still, by the mid–1960s, Elvis seemed stuck in a musical comedy rut. Elvis came to despise these films, partly because he never liked the genre to begin with and partly because **he wanted to be a serious actor.** However, there is no proof that Elvis would have been successful as a dramatic actor in the long term.

From top left: Flaming Star, Kid Galahad, *and* Wild in the Country

Famed pop artist **Andy Warhol** repeated a film still of Elvis in a series of silkscreens produced in the early 1960s. The still was taken from *Flaming Star*. These prints comment on the superficial nature of Hollywood stardom, and the repetition of the image suggests the lack of individual expression inherent in mass-produced art forms, such as the Hollywood movie or the silkscreen process. Interestingly, other artists took Warhol's famous silkscreen and expanded on it to create new pieces, including Richard Pettibone with *Andy Warhol, Elvis. 1964.* and Jerry Kearns with *Earth Angel.*

The use of Elvis imagery in fine art confirms that his impact on culture extends beyond the range of his own art. In life, Elvis blurred the line between black and white cultures with his music; in death, he blurs the line between high and low culture with his image.

MORE GREAT MOVIE TUNES

"Blue Hawaii" from *Blue Hawaii*

"Rock-a-Hula Baby"
- - - - from *Blue Hawaii*

"Follow That Dream" from
Follow That Dream

"Return to Sender" from
Girls! Girls! Girls!

"What'd I Say" from
Viva Las Vegas

"Viva Las Vegas" from
Viva Las Vegas

"Little Egypt" from *Roustabout*

"Drums of the Islands"
from *Paradise,*
Hawaiian Style

Follow That Dream

The title *Follow That Dream* suggests that it is another one of Elvis's romantic musical comedies. While there is music, romance, and comedy, the film differs from his other 1960s films because it was adapted from the satiric novel *Pioneer, Go Home* by Richard Powell. Powell's book is more complex than the film, but the script by Hollywood veteran Charles Lederer does feature some witty jabs at modern life.

The story follows the Kwimpers, a backwoods family who decide to homestead on a stretch of beach along a Florida highway, much to the chagrin of local officials. Elvis plays Toby Kwimper, the handsome oldest son who, despite being a bit dim-witted, manages to attract the attention of women. The Kwimpers are honest, simple folk who just don't understand the complexities of the modern world, which offers the film the opportunity to poke a bit of fun at everything from psychology to social bureaucracy.

Advertisements for Follow That Dream

FAVORITE DIALOGUE FROM ELVIS FLICKS

Toby (Elvis): I like girls alright, except when they start to bother me.

Alisha: Young virile man like you, I should think you'd like to be bothered.

Toby: The botherin' part is alright, but I ain't gonna marry no girl and build no house just so I can be bothered regular.

—*FOLLOW THAT DREAM*

Shooting on actual Florida beaches added a touch of authenticity to *Follow That Dream,* but location filming did give the producers minor headaches. The temperature soared past 100 degrees one week, making it difficult on the cast, crew, and equipment. Elvis had to change his shirt 22 times in one day because he was perspiring so much.

HOW GREAT THOU ART

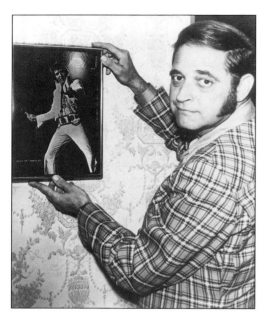

Felton Jarvis

Elvis went to RCA studios in Nashville in spring 1966 to make a gospel album, *How Great Thou Art.* As a child of the South, he was steeped in gospel music, and he especially liked the four-part harmony style sung by male gospel quartets associated with the shape note singing schools from the early 20th century. Elvis's favorite gospel quartets included the Blackwood Brothers, whom he knew personally, and the Statesmen, whose lead singer was the colorful Jake Hess. Elvis asked Hess and his new group, the Imperials, to join him on this album. *How Great Thou Art* proved to be a milestone in Elvis's career, winning him the first of his three Grammys, this one for Best Sacred Performance.

From January 1964 to May 1966, Elvis recorded nothing but movie soundtracks, mostly in Hollywood. Unsatisfied with his life for complex professional and personal reasons, he did not venture into the Nashville studios to cut any album material. When he finally decided to record new material, he returned to the studio with new musicians and a new producer, Felton Jarvis.

Jake Hess

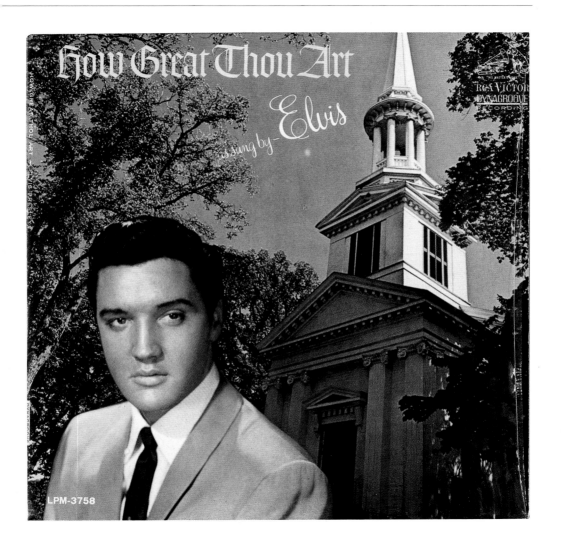

How Great Thou Art

as sung by Elvis

RCA VICTOR
DYNAGROOVE
RECORDING

LPM-3758

HOW GREAT THOU ART — ELVIS PRESLEY

213

THE WORST MOVIE TUNES

"No Room to Rhumba in a Sports Car"

from *Fun in Acapulco*

"Fort Lauderdale Chamber of Commerce"

from *Girl Happy*

"Do the Clam"

from *Girl Happy*

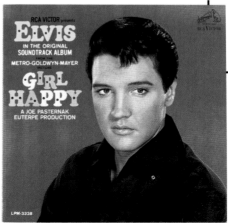

"Barefoot Ballad" from
Kissin' Cousins

"Yoga Is as Yoga Does" from
Easy Come, Easy Go

"He's Your Uncle, Not Your Dad" from *Speedway*

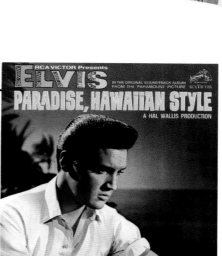

"Petunia, the Gardener's Daughter"
from *Frankie and Johnny*

"Queenie Wahini's Papaya" from *Paradise, Hawaiian Style*

Viva Las Vegas

When Elvis returned to Hollywood in July 1963 to begin work on *Viva Las Vegas,* little did he realize he was about to meet his on-screen match. Ann-Margret was a starlet on the rise when she agreed to costar in Elvis's fifteenth film. A singer-dancer, Ann-Margret injected the film's musical numbers with a vitality and professionalism that had been lacking in Elvis's films for some time. Elvis matched her youthful eagerness

with enthusiasm. It surprised no one when the on-screen sparks between Elvis and Ann-Margret ignited a passionate relationship offscreen as well. *Viva Las Vegas* was a critical and popular success.

It grossed the year. Reviews were generally good. One critic was more perceptive than most when he remarked, "For once everybody in the cast of an Elvis Presley picture isn't overshadowed by the rock 'n' roll hero." Colonel Tom Parker and Elvis's management team preferred that a Presley vehicle showcase only Elvis Presley. After *Viva Las Vegas*, Elvis would never again woo a leading lady with the talent and charisma of Ann-Margret—either on or off the screen.

FAVORITE DIALOGUE FROM ELVIS FLICKS

Rusty (Ann-Margret): I'd like you to check my motor. It whistles.

Lucky (Elvis): I don't blame it.

—*Viva Las Vegas*

Ann-Margret shared many things in common with Elvis, including the pressure of a show business career. Both enjoyed similar activities, such as riding motorcycles, and she got along well with members of Elvis's entourage. They called her "Rusty Ammo" or "Ann-Margrock."

DANCES

David Winters, who choreographed several Elvis films as well as the television series *Hullabaloo,* was asked to invent a dance for *Girl Happy.* Winters came up with the Clam, which was introduced in the song "Do the Clam." Unfortunately, the Clam did not catch on like other 1960s dance crazes such as the Pony, the Monkey, or the Jerk.

The Clam was not the only dance that was spotlighted in an Elvis Presley film. The Forte Four sing "The Climb" in *Viva Las Vegas*, with Elvis, Ann-Margret, and a group of teens performing the dance steps that went with the song. In *Blue Hawaii,* Elvis introduced a dance called Slicin' Sand with a song by the same name, but like the Clam, the dance did not catch on.

From top: The Climb, Slicin' Sand, and the Clam

Norman Taurog was responsible for nine Elvis Presley features—more than any other director. Elvis always favored Taurog, probably because of his kind nature and lack of ego. After particularly difficult scenes, the fatherly director would pass out candy bars to his cast and crew. Taurog was known primarily for lightweight vehicles and comedies, a specialty that dated all the way back to 1919 when his directorial career was launched with a series starring silent comedian Larry Semon. The consummate studio director, Taurog directed many major stars in more than 70 films across six decades. He won an Oscar in 1931 for Skippy, a vehicle for child star Jackie Cooper, and he was nominated again in 1938 for the classic *Boys Town*. Taurog died in 1981.

"I was always **proud of his work,** even if I wasn't proud of the scripts. I always felt that he never reached his peak."

—Norman Taurog

Small Parts for Big Actors

- **Christina Crawford,** Joan Crawford's daughter and author of *Mommie Dearest*, played Monica George in *Wild in the Country*.

Joan O'Brien, Elvis, and a young Kurt Russell

- **Charles Bronson,** a major action star of the 1970s, costarred as Lew Nyack in Kid Galahad. Also, a young **Ed Asner,** who played Lou Grant in two highly successful television series, made the most of a small role.

- **Kurt Russell,** who would later play Elvis in a made-for-TV film, appears as a kid who kicks Elvis in the shin in *It Happened at the World's Fair.*

- **Teri Garr,** the girl-next-door in several famous films of the 1980s, can claim the crown for appearing in bit parts in the most Elvis films. Look closely and you can see her as a dancer in *Viva Las Vegas, Roustabout,* and *Clambake,* and as an extra in *Kissin' Cousins* and *Fun in Acapulco.*

- **Richard Kiel,** who played Jaws in the James Bond film *The Spy Who Loved Me,* made a brief appearance as the carnival strong man in *Roustabout.* **Raquel Welch** also showed up, playing a college girl.

- **Dan Haggerty,** who enjoyed fame as the title character in TV's *Grizzly Adams,* played Charlie in *Girl Happy.*

- **Michael Murphy,** Michael Murphy, one of Woody Allen's key actors during the 1970s and the star of the innovative TV show *Tanner '88,* made his second screen appearance as Morley in *Double Trouble.*

- **Dabney Coleman,** everyone's favorite oily villain in such films as *9 to 5,* played Harrison Wilby in *The Trouble with Girls.*

- **Jane Elliot,** who has played Tracy Quartermaine on *General Hospital* for two decades, got her big break as Sister Barbara Bennett in *Change of Habit.*

A SINGING RACE-CAR DRIVER, PILOT, OR RODEO PERFORMER

Elvis's characters worked in a variety of colorful and romantic occupations, which was an expected part of his musical comedies. His most frequent occupation was as a performer of some kind, generally a singer, as in *Girl Happy* and *Double Trouble,* but he also played an actor in *Harum Scarum* and the manager of a chautauqua in *The Trouble with Girls.*

When he wasn't playing a performer, Elvis often played a race-car driver. He was a racer in *Viva Las Vegas, Spinout,* and *Speedway.* Other repeated occupations were an airplane pilot in *It Happened at the World's Fair,* and *Paradise, Hawaiian Style,* and a rodeo performer in *Tickle Me* and *Stay Away, Joe.* No matter how exotic the occupation (remember the trapeze artist-turned-lifeguard in *Fun in Acapulco*), his characters could always sing!

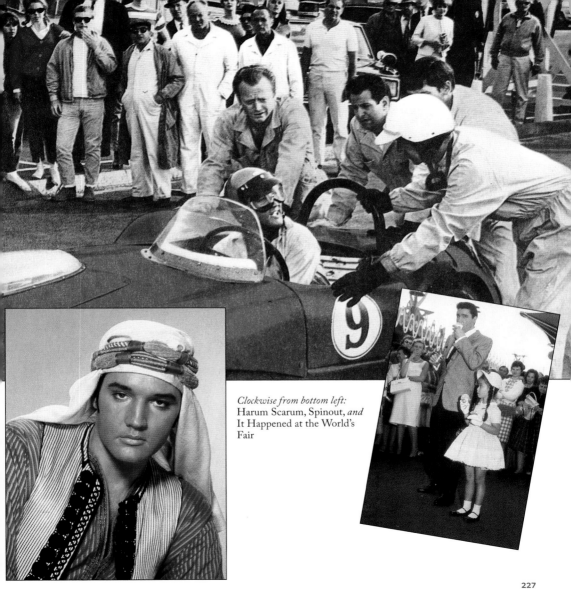

Clockwise from bottom left:
Harum Scarum, Spinout, *and*
It Happened at the World's
Fair

Charro!

With its gritty look, violent antihero, and cynical point of view, *Charro!* was obviously patterned after the grim Italian westerns of the 1960s. Elvis's character, Jess Wade, is costumed similarly to Clint Eastwood's notorious "Man with No Name" from Sergio Leone's Italian westerns. Both wore a scruffy beard and dust-covered western garb, and both kept a well-worn cigar in their mouths. The music in *Charro!* was scored by Hugh Montenegro, who was responsible for the memorable score of *The Good, the Bad, and the Ugly.* Unfortunately,

Charro! *was a departure from Elvis's usual musical comedies.*

director Charles Marquis Warren was no match for Sergio Leone, and *Charro!* suffers from poor production values.

At the time, much was made about the absence of songs in the film, as though that fact proved *Charro!* was a serious effort. Advertisements for the film declared that *Charro!* featured "a different kind of role . . . . a different kind of man." Elvis granted more interviews and generated more publicity for *Charro!* than he had for any film in a long time. One interview quoted

Ads for Charro! emphasized the difference from Elvis's other films.

him as saying "*Charro!* is the first movie I ever made without singing a song. I play a gunfighter, and I just couldn't see a singing gunfighter." Eventually, Elvis did agree to sing the title tune, but there are no songs within the body of the film.

ELVIS'S BEST COSTARS

Elvis worked with some of the best actors in Hollywood, past and present. Some were movie stars, some starlets, some character actors, and some veterans from another era, but all added depth and professionalism to the performances in the films.

Richard Egan in *Love Me Tender*

Walter Matthau and Carolyn Jones in *King Creole*

Juliet Prowse in *G.I. Blues*

Dolores Del Rio and John McIntire in *Flaming Star*

Angela Lansbury in *Blue Hawaii*

Gig Young in *Kid Galahad*

Tuesday Weld in

Wild in the Country - - - - - - - - - - - - - -

Arthur O'Connell in
Follow That Dream

Ann-Margret in *Viva Las Vegas*

Barbara Stanwyck in *Roustabout*

Sue Ane Langdon in
Frankie and Johnny

Joan Blondell in *Stay Away, Joe*

Mary Tyler Moore and

Jane Elliot in *Change of Habit* - - - - - - - - -

ELVIS'S FAVORITE *Costar*

Bubbly **Shelley Fabares** was supposedly Elvis's favorite costar. She appeared in *Girl Happy, Clambake*, and *Spinout*. A child actress, Fabares got her start on the TV sitcom *The Donna Reed Show*. She eventually returned to a career on the small screen.

No stranger to the pop music scene, Shelley Fabares had recorded "Johnny Angel," a number-one hit in 1962.

WHAT MIGHT HAVE BEEN

During the years that Elvis was an actor in Hollywood, he had several opportunities to star in films that were not "Presley travelogues," but these opportunities fell through. Often, the Colonel refused to agree to a film that did not follow the formula or did not showcase Elvis to his best advantage.

He turned down the 1956 rock 'n' roll spoof *The Girl Can't Help It,* because the money wasn't good enough and because Elvis would have had to share the screen with other notable rock 'n' roll acts. In the 1970s, Barbra Streisand was rumored to have wanted Elvis for her remake of *A Star Is Born,* but supposedly the Colonel turned her down. Kris Kristofferson played the role. Other roles that Elvis turned down included Hank Williams in *Your Cheatin' Heart* (George Hamilton played Williams) and the singing cowboy in *The Fastest Guitar in the West* (Roy Orbison got the part). Rumors persist that Elvis could have appeared in *Thunder Road, The Way to the Gold,* and *The Defiant Ones,* but these rumors may have been born of bitterness over Elvis's lost potential as an actor. Other factors

A Star Is Born

prevented Elvis from appearing in certain films, including the timing of projects and failed deals. Elvis was once set to play a James Bond-like superspy in a comedy adventure called *That Jack Valentine*, but the film was never produced. Other projects that fell through included a proposed musical starring Elvis opposite a classical artist and a comedy teaming Elvis with French legend Brigitte Bardot.

Thunder Road

THE FILMS OF ELVIS PRESLEY

Love Me Tender (1956)

Loving You (1957)

Jailhouse Rock (1957)

King Creole (1958)

G.I. Blues (1960)

Flaming Star (1960)

Wild in the Country (1961)

Blue Hawaii (1961)

Follow That Dream (1962)

Kid Galahad (1962)

Girls! Girls! Girls! (1962)

It Happened at the World's Fair (1963)

Fun in Acapulco (1963)

Kissin' Cousins (1964)

Viva Las Vegas (1964)

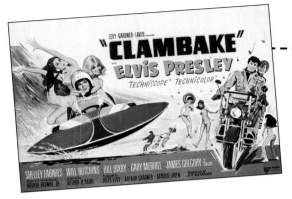

Clambake (1967)

Stay Away, Joe (1968)

Speedway (1968)

Live a Little, Love a Little (1968)

Charro! (1969)

The Trouble with Girls (1969)

Change of Habit (1969)

Elvis: That's the Way It Is (1970)

Elvis on Tour (1972)

Roustabout (1964)

Girl Happy (1965)

Tickle Me (1965)

Harum Scarum (1965)

Frankie and Johnny (1966)

Paradise, Hawaiian Style (1966)

Spinout (1966)

Easy Come, Easy Go
(1967)

Double Trouble (1967)

CONCERT KING

"Presley remains a true American artist—

one of the greatest in American popular music, a singer of native brilliance and a performer of magnetic dimensions."

—JIM MILLAR, ROLLING STONE

Energized by the positive reception for The '68 Comeback Special, Elvis **returned to the stage to perform** before a live audience. He tested the waters with an engagement at the International Hotel in Las Vegas in 1969, a critically acclaimed performance attended by the biggest celebrities of the day. Shortly thereafter, he hit the road again to tour the country. For the rest of his life, Elvis alternated between Vegas engagements and extensive touring. In his stage performances, Elvis was not content to sing the songs that made him famous during the 1950s. He did perform a medley of his old rockabilly classics in an updated arrangement, but his act was organized around contemporary tunes. Elvis had eclectic taste in music, a facet of his career that is generally underappreciated and rarely acknowledged. During the concert era, he featured country, pop, rhythm-and-blues, and rock, moving easily from one genre to another without missing a beat. Impossible to classify as a singer and influenced only by the quality of a song, Elvis Presley refused to be bound by a single genre—or by musical limits of any kind.

Left: Loving You
Above: Stay Away, Joe
Right: King Creole

With this witty quip, Elvis effectively summed up his opinion on his film career and explained his renewed focus on music: "I get tired of playing a guy who gets into a fight, then starts singing to the guy he's just beat up."

—*NEWSWEEK*, AUGUST 11, 1969

The '68 Comeback Special

In early 1968, Colonel Tom Parker closed a deal for Elvis to appear in his own television special for NBC. It was taped in late June and aired on December 3. The Colonel's vision of the special had Elvis walking in front of a Christmas tree, singing favorite familiar carols, and then wishing everyone a happy holiday.

However, Steve Binder, the producer of the special, had a different vision. He hoped to capture what he felt was Elvis's genius—the adaptation of rhythm-and-blues to the tastes of mainstream audiences. He wanted to prove that Elvis was not a relic of rock 'n' roll's past.

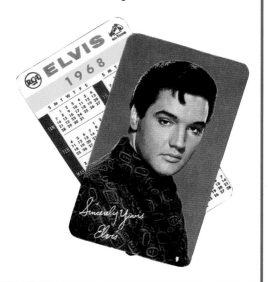

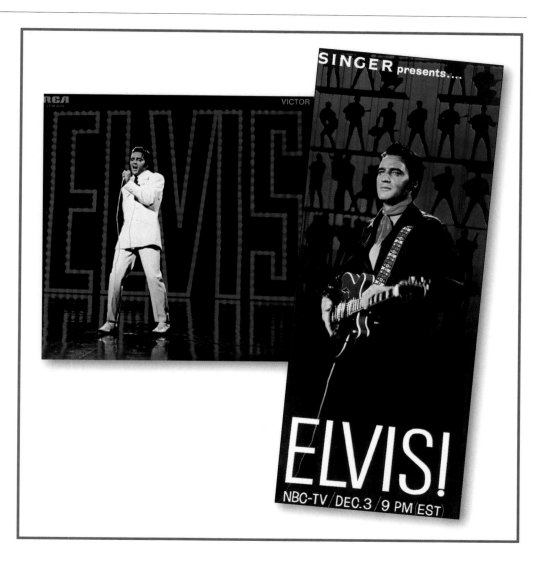

JUST the Facts

The Making of a Comeback

- The original name of The '68 Comeback Special was simply *Elvis*. It aired on December 3, 1968.

- The special was sponsored by Singer Sewing Machines, and some of the promotional material refers to it as *Singer Presents Elvis.*

- Elvis wore a gold lamé jacket while performing "Trouble," which echoed his famous lamé suit from 1958 without exactly duplicating it. The approach was meant to remind viewers of the pre-movie Elvis without making him a carbon copy of the past.

- In the concert segment, Elvis and four musicians sat on a small stage and reminisced about the past while performing updated versions of Elvis hits. Two of those musicians were Scotty Moore and D. J. Fontana, two-thirds of the Blue Moon Boys.

- The special received a 32 rating and a 42 share, making it the highest rated program the week that it was broadcast.

The '68 Comeback Special closed with the moving spiritual **"If I Can Dream."** The song was written at the last minute at the request of the show's producer, Steve Binder. The musical director of The '68 Comeback Special, W. Earl Brown, wrote the song as a response to the assassinations of Robert Kennedy and Martin Luther King, Jr. It was intended as a statement of hope for the future. Elvis loved "If I Can Dream," and he gave it all he had.

The instrumental track was recorded on June 20 or 21, 1968. Elvis sang the song in front of the orchestra's string section while the instrumental part was being recorded. Though his vocals were not to be used on the final version, he sang with all the passion the song inspired, even dropping down on his knee at one point. The effect left the string section with their mouths agape. Later, Elvis rerecorded the vocals in a darkened studio, and once again, he performed the song rather than merely recording it.

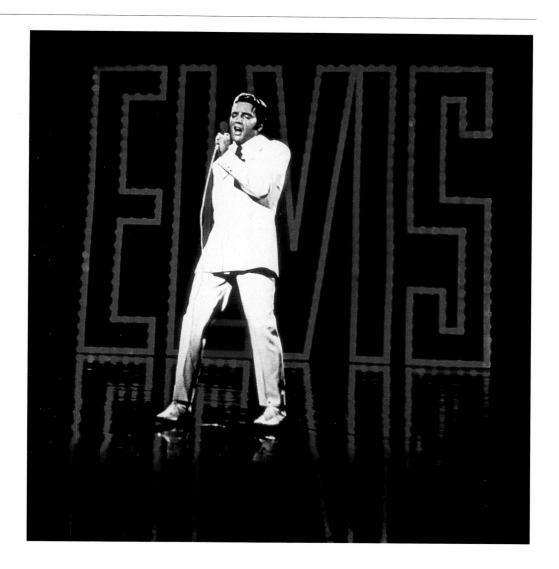

"There is something special about **watching a man who has lost himself find his way back home.** He sang with the kind of power people no longer associate with rock 'n' roll singers. He moved his body with a lack of pretension and effort that must have made Jim Morrison green with envy. And while most of the songs were ten or twelve years old, he performed them as freshly as though they were written yesterday."

—Rock critic Jon Landau on *The '68 Comeback Special*

Inspired and invigorated by the success of his television special, Elvis walked through the door of tiny American Sound Studios in Memphis in January 1969 to make quality music that would garner him hit records. Elvis had not recorded in his hometown since he left Sun in 1955, but the musical atmosphere at RCA's Nashville studios had become stale. His friends and associates encouraged him to record at American Sound because Nashville would yield nothing for him at this time.

American Sound Studios, a small studio in a run-down neighborhood, was operated by Chips Moman. With Moman as producer, Elvis worked hard to record his first significant mainstream album in years. In retrospect, **From Elvis in Memphis** may be his most important album because it brought his recording career back from soundtrack purgatory and set a creative standard for the next few years. No longer the crooning movie star, Elvis had returned to the music scene to reclaim his crown as the

King of Rock 'n' Roll.
The house band at
American Sound Studios
included musicians who
were steeped in all forms
of Southern music.
Both Black and White
artists recorded at
American Sound, and
the house band was
generally the same no matter
who recorded there. Many of these
musicians, including guitarist Reggie
Young, bassist Tommy Cogbill, and
pianist Bobby Wood, grew up

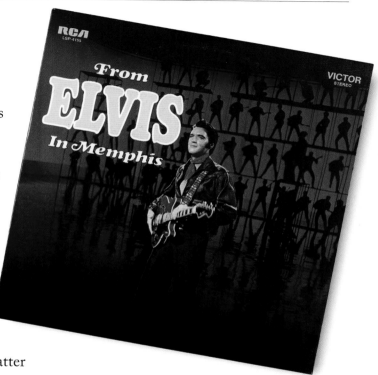

listening to
Elvis's music. No more fitting group
of musicians could have backed Elvis
on his return to Memphis.

A RETURN TO THE STAGE
LAS VEGAS, JULY 31, 1969

After the benefit for the USS *Arizona* at Bloch Arena at Pearl Harbor in 1961, Elvis did not perform before a live audience for more than eight years. Invigorated by his 1968 television special and his first major album in years, *From Elvis in Memphis*, he accepted an offer to perform in the new 2,000-seat showroom of the International Hotel in Las Vegas (later the Hilton). Barbra Streisand had opened the room the previous month, and Elvis attended her closing night. Elvis had rehearsed for a month with his new band, and despite a few glitches, the audience of celebrities and reporters responded to his opening night with a standing ovation. In his new act, Elvis performed a medley of his greatest hits but also included new material from his recent recording sessions in Memphis. Reviews of his nearly sold-out engagement were positive. Total attendance exceeded 101,509, which was a Vegas record, as was the $1,522,635 box-office take.

THE CONCERT BAND

A consequence of Elvis's new direction in the 1970s was a change in the core group of musicians who recorded and toured with him. Chief among these musicians was lead guitarist James Burton, who had worked with Ricky Nelson. An accomplished and respected lead guitar player, Burton later worked with Gram Parsons and Emmylou Harris. Other band members included several Hollywood session musicians who had occasionally contributed to Elvis's movie soundtracks: bassist Jerry Scheff, who had worked with the Doors; pianist Larry Muhoberac; and drummer Ronnie Tutt. Elvis's new sound was large-scale, almost operatic. In addition to musicians, he used a male gospel quartet and a female backup group in his recording sessions and on the road. At first the Imperials gospel quartet, with the legendary Jake Hess, backed Elvis vocally, but later J. D. Sumner and the Stamps Quartet took over that role. The Sweet Inspirations fulfilled the duties as female backup voices, and Kathy Westmoreland supplied an additional soprano voice.

Guitarist James Burton (left) and drummer Ronnie Tutt (below) toured with Elvis in the 1970s.

257

ELVIS AND CHRISTMAS

Christmas was Elvis's favorite time of year, which is reflected by the many holiday singles and albums that he recorded over the years.

October 1971

November 1957

November 1965

December 1971

Throughout his life, Elvis loved celebrating the Christmas season with family and friends. In this 1957 photo, Elvis shows off a few of his holiday gifts.

Elvis's last number-one single, **"Suspicious Minds,"** offers an example of the large-scale sound that defined his later style. At four minutes and 22 seconds, it is his longest number-one song, and in his Las Vegas shows, he stretched it into a powerhouse, showstopping piece that ran eight minutes. Elvis had introduced the song in Vegas on July 26, 1969, when he made his first live performance at the International Hotel. It was not released as a single until the following September. The song entered Billboard's Hot 100 chart, peaking at the number-one position seven weeks later.

The song was originally recorded at American Sound Studios in Memphis on January 23, 1969, though it was held for release until a later date. "Suspicious Minds" featured backing vocals by Jeannie Green and Ronnie Milsap, a singer-songwriter who later became a prominent country-western star in his own right. To help achieve that large-scale sound, Elvis's Las Vegas band was overdubbed at a Vegas recording studio in August. Also, the end of the song was spliced on for a second time. This overdubbing and remixing was supervised by Elvis's producer, Felton Jarvis.

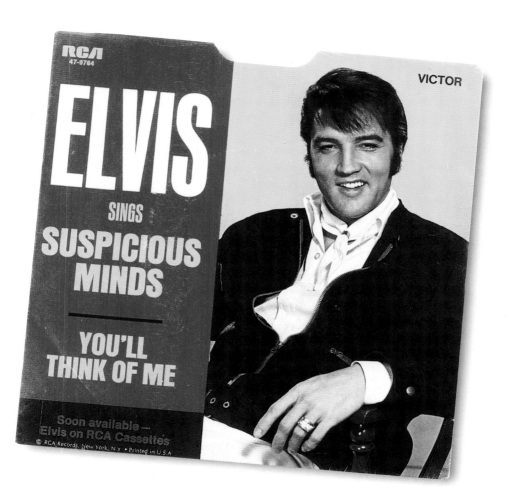

RCA
47-9764

VICTOR

ELVIS
SINGS
SUSPICIOUS MINDS

—

YOU'LL THINK OF ME

Soon available —
Elvis on RCA Cassettes

© RCA Records. New York, N.Y. • Printed in U.S.A.

261

ALMOST AS FAMOUS AS ELVIS

During his lifetime, Elvis respected the talent of many other performers and celebrities, even if their styles or arena of performance differed from his.

"One night I went into the casino after the show, and I saw [Bobby Darin] standing there with Elvis Presley . . . . both of them were **beautiful, polite, talented kids.** I thought I'd make them laugh. So . . . . I whispered, 'I see you fellows are alone. If you need any help meeting girls, don't be embarrassed to ask me.' Presley thought I was serious. 'Thank you, Mr. Burns,' he said. Toughest audience I ever worked to."

—GEORGE BURNS, REPRINTED IN
ELVIS! THE LAST WORD, 1991

Elvis and Bobby Darin

Tom Jones, Priscilla, and Elvis

Elvis and Liberace

Muhammad Ali and Elvis

Best Reinvented Songs by Elvis

"That's All Right" was written and recorded by Arthur "Big Boy" Crudup as a country blues tune in 1947 and reworked by Elvis in 1955. Elvis's fast-paced, rockabilly interpretation became his first single release.

Elvis recorded two versions of the Dave Bartholomew–Pearl King blues tune "One Night of Sin," which had been a hit for Smiley Lewis in 1956. On January 24, 1957, he recorded the Smiley Lewis version, and a month later he re-recorded the song as "One Night," using cleaned-up lyrics. In Lewis's risqué original, the singer is praying for "One night of sin," while in Elvis's more hopeful rendition of the song, he is simply yearning for "One night with you."

The Tin Pan Alley songwriters Lou Handman and Roy Turk composed "Are You Lonesome Tonight?" ("To-night" on the original record

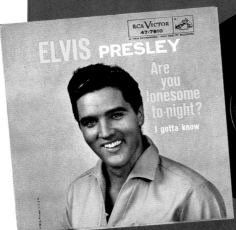

sleeve) in 1926, and it was originally recorded by Al Jolson the following year. Supposedly the only song Colonel Tom Parker ever urged Elvis to record, "Are You Lonesome Tonight?" was released by Elvis in 1960 and was later nominated for three Grammys.

Elvis sang James Taylor's 1970 composition "Steamroller Blues" in concert during the early 1970s, but his gritty rendition during the *Aloha from Hawaii* television special stopped the show. The version from the special was released as a single in April 1973.

"My Way," an anthem of independence and individuality, was written by Paul Anka for Frank Sinatra and originally recorded by Sinatra in 1969. Elvis sang "My Way" on the *Aloha from Hawaii* television special and in concert during the 1970s. A recording of this song by Elvis was released shortly after he died, making it something of a biographical statement.

THE ASTRODOME
HOUSTON, TEXAS
FEBRUARY 27–MARCH 1, 1970

Elvis's Las Vegas engagements in August 1969 and February 1970 represented his return to live performances, but his three-day gig at the Houston Astrodome launched his return to touring. The show was part of the Texas Livestock Show and Rodeo, and Elvis held two press conferences in conjunction with his engagement. At one, he acknowledged the importance of country music to his career and told reporters he was happy that it had gained in popularity. Though significant in terms of his career, the Astrodome engagement was not his best work, mainly due to problems with the equipment and microphones. Local reviews were positive, but they noted that the Astrodome was not the best place to see any type of musical concert. It was an enormous arena that even Elvis found somewhat intimidating. Still, his six shows drew 207,494 people.

From 1963 through 1980, **RCA Records** printed **pocket calendars** with Elvis's picture on one side and a 12-month calendar on the other. To promote goodwill, as well as Elvis's singles and albums, RCA issued the calendars to fan clubs and to record stores as giveaways for their customers.

Versions of the calendars were printed for foreign markets as well,

including Germany and Japan. The promotion proved to be a popular one, particularly after Elvis died. The rarest and most valuable calendar is the 1963 issue, while those from the years 1976 to 1980 are worth less than any others. In 1980, RCA celebrated 25 years of releasing Elvis Presley records. They issued authentic reproductions of all 18 calendars for individuals who ordered the 25th anniversary limited edition Elvis Presley box set. The reproductions feature small imperfections and differences, making it possible to spot the reissues.

Outstanding Young Man of America

On January 16, 1971, Elvis Presley was named one of the Ten Outstanding Young Men of America by the Junior Chamber of Commerce (Jaycees), a nationally based community group devoted to civic duty. Each year, the Jaycees nominate young men, usually under the age of 30, who are praiseworthy in their fields. A panel of distinguished judges makes the final selection of ten. The judges, including former President Lyndon B. Johnson, chose Elvis not only because he was the greatest entertainer of his time but also because of his many acts of philanthropy and charity. Visitors who see the Jaycees award at Graceland cannot help but notice the scuff and scratch marks. Elvis carried the statue with him on every tour and trip until he died.

With Priscilla by his side, Elvis is honored by the Jaycees.

"I learned very early in life that without a song, the day would never end; **without a song, a man ain't got a friend;** without a song, the road would never bend—without a song. So I keep singing a song."

—ELVIS, ON ACCEPTING THE JAYCEES' OUTSTANDING YOUNG MAN OF AMERICA AWARD

ELVIS DROPS IN ON A PRESIDENT

In December 1970, Elvis made a decision to travel to Washington, D.C., to visit Deputy U.S. Narcotics Director John Finlator. Although Elvis said that he was going to volunteer his help in the antidrug campaign, he was actually hoping to obtain a federal narcotics badge to add to his collection. Finlator turned down Elvis's request for a badge, but Elvis decided to go over Finlator's head. With a couple of members of the Memphis Mafia, Elvis called on President Richard Nixon at the White House. The charismatic Presley was able to talk Nixon into giving him an authentic narcotics agent's badge in a matter of minutes.

On later trips, Elvis visited FBI headquarters to offer his assistance in fighting the war on drugs. While it's not surprising that Elvis visited law-enforcement agencies, the fact that he could get in to see the president on a few hours' notice is testimony to Elvis's popularity and power. Other entertainers have been honored by invitations to perform at the White House, but the King simply dropped in to get something he wanted.

Elvis's 32nd film, ***Elvis: That's the Way It Is,*** was not a narrative feature but a documentary showcasing his 1970 summer appearance at the International Hotel in Las Vegas. Elvis began rehearsals July 5 at the MGM studios in Hollywood, where he worked on his material for about a month. The show opened August 10. The MGM cameras not only recorded the rehearsals but also opening night, several performances throughout the engagement, and one show at Veterans Memorial Coliseum in Phoenix, Arizona. The film is structured so that the rehearsals and other scenes of preparation build to an extended climax of Elvis onstage. Performing in a simple white jumpsuit accented with fringe instead of rhinestones and gems, Elvis is captured at the pinnacle of his career.

Souvenir
Folio
Concert
Edition

Volume Six

"A live concert to me **is exciting** because of all the electricity that is generated in the crowd and on stage. It's my favorite part of the business—live concerts."

—ELVIS, 1973

The highlight of Elvis's studio sessions during March 1972 was the recording of **"Burning Love."** By this point, Elvis and his band were masters of this type of large-scale, fast-rocking number, and his interpretation of the song typifies his 1970s sound.

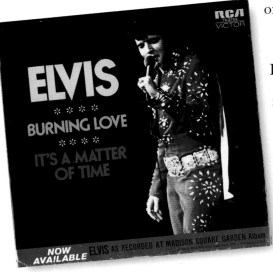

Dennis Linde composed "Burning Love" and played guitar on the recording. It was Linde who dubbed in the raucous guitar lick on the bridges of the song. He had occasionally served as a bass guitarist in Elvis's recording band during the 1970s.

"Burning Love" became a worldwide hit for Elvis in 1972, and it quickly charted on *Billboard's* Hot 100. Peaking at number two, it just missed becoming a number-one record. Chuck Berry's "My Ding-a-Ling" kept "Burning Love" from hitting the top of the charts. The record was certified gold by the RIAA in October 1972, and it was certified platinum in March 1992.

"Burning Love" Jumpsuit

Elvis wore a bright red jumpsuit onstage during his fall tour in 1972. The costume quickly became a fan favorite and one of his most famous stage costumes. Fans began referring to it as the "Burning Love" jumpsuit, perhaps because of its color. Also, the song "Burning Love" was included in set lists for his tour that year. Confusion exists about the "Burning Love" jumpsuit because the white costume and cape worn onstage at the Madison Square Garden engagement in June 1972 had once been given the same name. Elvis appears in the white suit on the cover of the album *Burning Love and Hits from His Movies, Volume 2,* which is why that costume had originally been christened "Burning Love." However, the title seemed better suited to the red stage costume, and over time, the red suit usurped the cherished nickname. Elvis donated the red suit to the National Cerebral Palsy Telethon in 1972. In October 1995, the suit was sold at a Las Vegas auction for a record $107,000.

Elvis performs in the "Burning Love" jumpsuit.

MADISON SQUARE GARDEN
JUNE 9–11, 1972

Elvis Presley made entertainment history with his four-show engagement at Madison Square Garden. He was the first performer to sell out all of his shows in advance, grossing about $730,000. A total of 80,000 people attended his performances, including John Lennon, David Bowie, Bob Dylan, and George Harrison. During the engagement, Elvis wore sequined jumpsuits and gold-lined capes, which by 1972 was typical for his concert performances. The Sweet Inspirations, J. D. Sumner and the Stamps Quartet, and Elvis's touring band backed him. The act included a medley of his classic hits, during which he engaged in some self-parody to the delight of the audience. He also performed new material, including the very Southern "An American Trilogy," a song that mystified the New York critics. Remarkably, the engagement marked the first time Elvis had ever given a live concert in New York City.

Jerry Weintraub in Association with RCA Records Tours Presents

JUNE 9-10 AT

madison square garden
Pennsylvania Plaza-7th Ave., 31st to 33rd Sts.

DON'T MISS IT

FRIDAY NIGHT	SATURDAY MATINEE	SATURDAY NIGHT
June 9-8:30 P.M.	**June 10-2:30** P.M.	**June 10-8:30** P.M.
	Prices:	Prices:
$10, $7.50, $5. Tax incl.	**$10, $7.50, $5.** Tax incl.	**$10, $7.50, $5.** Tax incl.

Tickets on sale Monday, May 8th, at Madison Square Garden
For additional information, call (212) 564-4400. Tickets also available at Ticketron outlets
in these cities: New York (212) 644-4400, Boston (617) 655-5440, Philadelphia (215) LO 3-9008,
Pittsburgh (412) 922-5300, Washington, D.C. (202) 659-2601.

NO MAIL ORDERS ACCEPTED.
Hear Elvis on RCA Records and Tapes.

"Elvis ....
materialized in a white
suit of lights, shining
with golden appliques,
the shirt front slashed to
show his chest. Around
his shoulders was a cape
lined in a cloth of gold,
its collar faced with
scarlet. It was anything
you wanted to call it,
**gaudy, vulgar—
magnificent.**

—*THE NEW YORK TIMES*,
JUNE 10, 1972,
MADISON SQUARE GARDEN
OPENING NIGHT

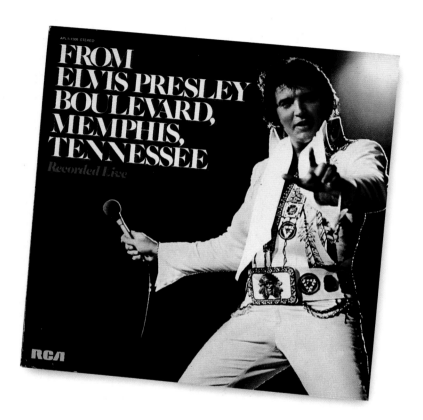

"Ask anyone. If it hadn't been for Elvis, I don't know where popular music would be. **He was the one that started it all off,** and he was definitely the start of it for me."

—ELTON JOHN

Elvis as Recorded at Madison Square Garden

- RCA recorded all four concerts at Elvis's famous engagement at Madison Square Garden in June 1972.

- The performance from June 10 was used for this album.

- Eager to take advantage of the good press for this series of concerts, which marked the first time Elvis ever played a live engagement in New York City, RCA had the album produced, the records pressed, and the product in stores less than two weeks later.

- The album was certified gold by the RIAA on August 4, 1972.

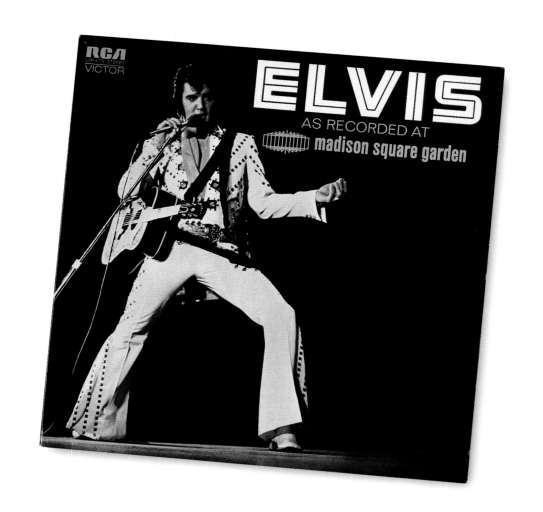

Elvis on Tour

The second documentary to capture Elvis in performance focused on his road show. *Elvis on Tour* followed the singer's 15-city tour in the spring of 1972. The tour started in Buffalo, New York, and came to a rousing conclusion in Albuquerque, New Mexico. Much of the tour centered in the South, where Elvis's popularity reached a peak in the 1970s.

In addition to the footage of Elvis in concert, the film attempted to reveal the real Elvis Presley backstage and off-guard. A camera followed the singer and his entourage, while Elvis was asked to comment on such topics as his music and childhood. According to filmmakers Pierre Adidge and Robert Abel in the film press kit, ". . . . after we filmed [Elvis] on tour and were allowed to shoot and record in places he had never allowed cameras in the past, we finally asked if he would mind talking about himself. He thought awhile and finally agreed." Despite a few humorous candid moments, however, these interviews did not reveal the real Elvis but only added to the myth that surrounded him.

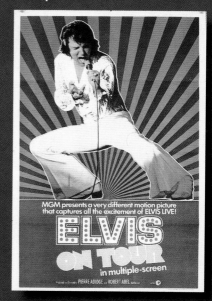

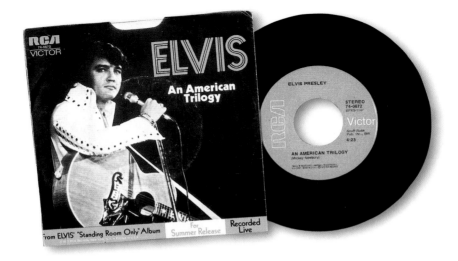

Originally arranged and recorded by country singer Mickey Newbury, **"An American Trilogy"** is a medley of "Dixie," "The Battle Hymn of the Republic," and "All My Trials." The integration of two Civil War songs (one a Southern anthem, the other a Northern anthem) with a traditional spiritual suggests the curiously Southern tradition of blending diverse cultural elements. Elvis's 1972 version of the piece offered an operatic interpretation that matched the breadth of the song's meaning.

In 1968, country singer Marty Robbins wrote **"You Gave Me a Mountain,"** a wrenching ballad about life's hardships. Though pop star Frankie Laine was the first to release it, Elvis began singing the song in concert during the early 1970s and released it in 1973. Elvis's interpretation is generally considered autobiographical in that it paralleled his breakup with Priscilla Presley.

ELVIS'S FAVORITE SNACK
PEANUT BUTTER AND BANANA SANDWICH

- 3 tablespoons peanut butter

- 2 slices of light bread*

- 1 banana, mashed

- 2 tablespoons margarine, melted

Mix soft peanut butter and mashed banana together. Toast bread lightly. Spread peanut butter and mashed banana on toast. Place into melted margarine in skillet; brown on both sides.

* The recipe is referring to homemade baked bread, not bread that is light in calories.

"The image is one thing and the human being is another .... **it's very hard to live up to an image.**"

—ELVIS PRESLEY,
PRESS CONFERENCE FOR MADISON SQUARE GARDEN SHOW,
JUNE 1972

Elvis: Aloha from Hawaii

was beamed by the Intelsat IV satellite to countries all over the world on January 14, 1973. Broadcast at 12:30 A.M. Hawaii time, the special was seen in Australia, New Zealand, the Philippine Islands, Japan, and other countries in Asia. Even parts of communist China

supposedly tuned in. The next day, the show was rebroadcast to 28 European countries. The special consisted of a concert performance by Elvis in front of a live audience at the Honolulu International Convention Center. After the audience left the arena, Elvis was filmed singing five more songs, which were to be included in the U.S. edition of the concert. NBC's broadcast of the show on April 4 included only four of the additional songs, however. The U.S. broadcast of the special was watched by 51 percent of the television viewing audience—more than watched the first walk on the moon.

ALOHA FROM HAWAII JUMPSUIT

Elvis wanted a costume that signified America for Aloha from Hawaii, so designer Bill Belew produced a white jumpsuit with an American eagle patterned in red, gold, and blue gems. The costume's spectacular calf-length cape proved to be too cumbersome during rehearsals, so Elvis ordered a hip-length cape to replace it. A belt decorated with gold American eagles accented the ensemble.

During the show, Elvis threw the belt and the cape into the cheering crowd. Elvis ordered a second cape and belt for the jumpsuit and wore the outfit in later performances. The original belt has never surfaced, and

the original cape is now in the hands of a private collector. By the end of 1974, Elvis stopped wearing capes onstage. Not only were they heavy and uncomfortable, but members of the audience tended to grab the edges of them while he was performing, resulting in some near accidents.

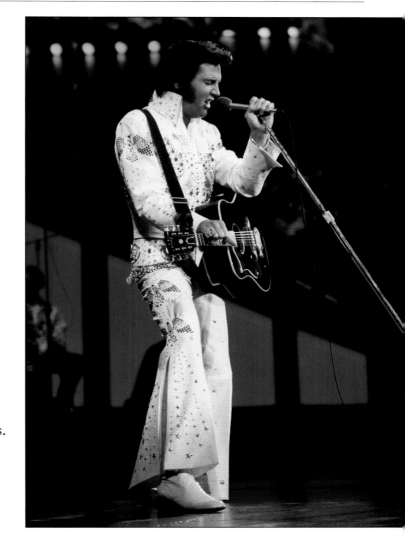

MASTER OF THE JUMPSUIT

Bill Belew was the tailor who designed Elvis's concert costumes, beginning in 1968 when he created the black leather suit for The '68 Comeback Special. Though most associate the white jumpsuit with this phase of Elvis's career, there was quite a variety to Elvis's outfits. Some costumes were not jumpsuits at all, such as the black mohair suit Elvis wore at the International in 1969. The jumpsuits themselves came in a variety of colors and designs.

*American Eagle
1974*

Black Phoenix 1975

Black Conquistador 1972

Blue Rainbow 1974

The Peacock 1974

Green Cisco Kid
1971

Tiffany 1972

Indian Feather
1975

Grammy Awards

Despite his immeasurable impact on 20th-century popular music, Elvis won only three Grammy Awards during his lifetime. The Grammy, the most prestigious award in the music industry, was particularly coveted during Elvis's lifetime because there were far fewer music awards then. In 1967, Elvis won a Grammy for Best Sacred Performance for the album *How Great Thou Art*. Five years later, he won for Best Inspirational Performance for *He Touched Me*. In 1974, he won Best Inspirational Performance for the song "How Great Thou Art" from the album Elvis *Recorded Live* on *Stage in Memphis*. Because gospel music played such an important role in Elvis's life, he was especially gratified that he won for his inspirational recordings. In addition to his three awards, Elvis was nominated for Grammys ten times during his career. Also, the cover of *For LP Fans Only* was nominated for Best Album Cover in 1959.

FINAL ACT

From the day Elvis Presley passed away on August 16, 1977, the fans refused to let his legacy or his talent be forgotten. Despite the rumors that belittled his image and the real-life revelations that shocked the public, Elvis's fans remain loyal—even in the face of a caustic media that still prefers to paint Elvis fans as fanatics. The result is that new generations have become Elvis fans.

But Elvis was more than just a popular performer—his decades-long career, many shifts in his public image, and associations with such ideas as rebellion, sex, excess, and tragedy have rendered him an iconic or mythic figure. The Elvis legend is frequently evoked in movies, plays, and the songs of other musicians to convey an idea or make a point.

After his death, leadership at RCA focused on repackaging Elvis's music to emphasize its historical and musical significance. Their efforts have reinforced the idea that the true legacy of Elvis Presley is his music.

The King Is Dead

When Elvis Presley died on a hot August day in 1977, it made international headlines. From tiny Tupelo, Mississippi, to the glamorous boulevards of Paris, the world slowed down for a moment to mourn.

_ _ _"All Roads Lead to Memphis"

—*London Evening Standard*, August 17, 1977

"The King Is Dead"

—*Tupelo Daily Journal*, August 17, 1977

"A Lonely Life Ends on Elvis Presley Boulevard"

—*MEMPHIS PRESS-SCIMITAR*, AUGUST 17, 1977

"L'adieu à Elvis"

—*FRANCE-SOIR*, AUGUST 17, 1977

"Last Stop on the Mystery Train"

—*TIME*, AUGUST 29, 1977

"Elvis Has Left the Building"

—*STEREO REVIEW*, JANUARY 1978

"But it's hard to imagine Elvis Presley's success coming anywhere but here. He molded it out of so many American elements: country and blues and gospel and rock; a little Memphis, a little Vegas, a little arrogance, a little piety . . . . How could we ever have felt estranged from Elvis? **He was a native son.**"

—CHARLES KURALT, CBS NEWS SPECIAL, AUGUST 18, 1977

BEST
Collectibles

Unused Concert Tickets

Elvis was scheduled to leave on another grinding road trip on August 17, 1977. In poor physical shape, he was not looking forward to the tour, at least according to some of those around him. He had just completed a tour in June of that year, with his last performance at Market Square Arena in Indianapolis, Indiana, on June 26. Around 2:00 p.m. on August 16, Elvis Presley was found dead at Graceland. Many of the shows on the tour that never happened were already sold out. After Elvis's death, promoters offered a refund to ticket buyers. Many fans chose not to return their tickets, keeping them as souvenirs. The fans' reluctance to receive refunds caused confusion for promoters who had to account for their losses and pay cancellation fees. Later, many fans decided to sell their tickets for several times the face value.

Graceland

- Elvis's mansion in Memphis was opened to the public on June 7, 1982, and soon became one of the most visited homes in America.

- Each year, approximately 650,000 visitors come through the music gates to view the sights at Graceland. The home averages more than 1,750 visitors daily and, over the course of an eight-hour day, nearly 225 visitors per hour.

- Graceland has 23 rooms, including 8 bedrooms and 4½ baths.

- When the estate decided to open Graceland, Priscilla Presley replaced the red decor in the dining room with the blue, white, and gold color scheme from the 1960s, when she lived in the mansion. The red crushed-velvet furniture, red shag carpet, and red drapes were the result of a redecoration done in 1974 by Elvis's girlfriend, Linda Thompson.

- The three televisions in the TV room were inspired by something Elvis had read about Lyndon B. Johnson, who reportedly liked to watch the news on all three networks simultaneously. Instead of the news, Elvis was likely to watch three football games or other sporting events at once.

lIn 1991, Graceland was placed on the National Register of Historic Places.

I'VE BEEN INSIDE GRACELAND

Top Ten Sights at Graceland

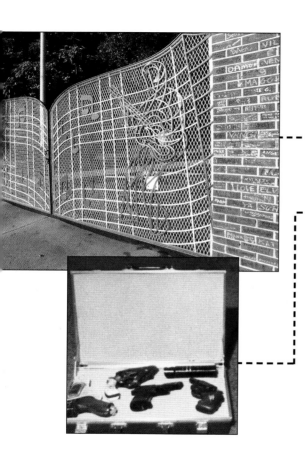

1. Music gates

2. Hall of Gold

3. Firearms collection

4. Badge collection

5. Elvis's record collection

6. RCA display of gold and platinum records

7. Meditation Garden

8. Elvis's jet, the *Lisa Marie*

9. The pink Cadillac Elvis bought for his mother

10. Wedding dress and suit

"There have been a lotta tough guys. There have been pretenders. There have been contenders. **But there is only one King."**

—BRUCE SPRINGSTEEN

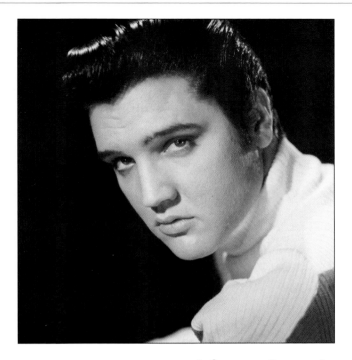

"Elvis was and remained **a working class hero,** a man who rose from obscurity and transformed American popular art in answer to his own needs—and who may have possibly been destroyed by the isolation that being an American celebrity sometimes entails. He was as much a metaphor as a maker of music, and one of telling power and poignancy."

—JOHN ROCKWELL, *THE NEW YORK TIMES*

"Elvis Presley's death deprives our country of a part of itself. **He was unique and irreplaceable.** More than 20 years ago, he burst upon the scene with an impact that was unprecedented and will probably never be equaled. His music and his personality, fusing the styles of White country and Black rhythm-and-blues, changed the face of American popular culture. His following was immense, and he was a symbol to people the world over of the vitality, rebelliousness, and good humor of his country."

—JIMMY CARTER,
AUGUST 17, 1977

TRIBUTE WEEK

Elvis's grave site at Graceland

Each year on the anniversary of Elvis's death, thousands of fans make the pilgrimage to Memphis to commemorate the life and career of Elvis Presley. Tribute Week began unofficially the first year after Elvis's death when fans showed up in mid-August and mingled outside the music gates at Graceland. That same year, Colonel Tom Parker, with Vernon Presley in tow, held a tribute called "Always Elvis" in Las Vegas. The Colonel's event drew little interest from the fans, however, and he never organized another.

Currently, Tribute Week consists of seven days of activities, memorials, and gatherings. Fans visit Graceland, Humes Junior High School, Sun Studio, Beale Street, and lesser-known Presley haunts such as Lauderdale Courts. The city welcomes the Elvis fans, who have helped turn Memphis into a thriving tourist mecca. Other activities include Elvis trivia contests, impersonator contests, collectibles conventions, and book signings by Elvis biographers.

During tribute week, the Meditation Garden is a sea of flowers.

The emotional high point of Tribute Week is the **candlelight vigil.** This ritual has been enacted in some form or another every year since Elvis's death. On the evening of August 15, fans gather in front of the music gates at Graceland. Elvis's music is piped over a loudspeaker as people mingle and swap Elvis stories before lining up along the graffiti-covered wall. At 11:00 P.M., two or more Graceland employees walk down to the gates with a torch that has been lit from the eternal flame that marks Elvis's grave. As the gates open, the fans, each with their own lighted candle, climb silently and reverently up the hill behind the house, where they walk single file past the grave site. The procession often takes as long as six hours to pass through the Meditation Garden. It is not only a gesture of respect for Elvis, but it is proof that Elvis's fans are as faithful after his death as they were during his lifetime.

Shortly after Elvis died, Hollywood turned its attention to the singer once again, realizing that his enormous popularity had not been diminished by death. In 1979, ABC aired the first of several films on the life of Elvis Presley. Directed by John Carpenter, ***Elvis, The Movie,*** was a solid attempt to encapsulate the singer's contributions to popular music as well as to sympathetically portray Elvis the man. Kurt Russell starred as Elvis in a powerful portrayal that garnered Russell an Emmy nomination.

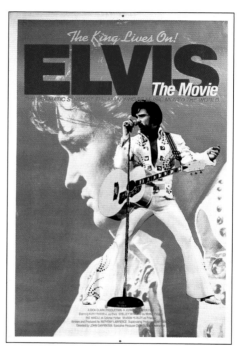

Produced, directed, and written by Andrew Solt and Malcolm Leo, *This Is Elvis* combines news footage, television performances, still photography, and re-created scenes to tell the story of Elvis's life and career. The film opens with the shocking news of the singer's death and then flashes back to his childhood years in Tupelo, Mississippi. Four different actors portray Elvis at various points in his life, including his teen years when he performs in front of his high school class for a talent show, his mature years when he is hospitalized for numerous ailments,

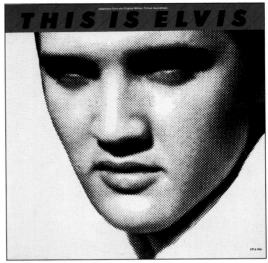

and on the eve of his death at Graceland. Other events and phases of his career are depicted through news footage, home movies, concert material, and still photography. Released in 1981, *This Is Elvis* was one of the first serious, if biased, examinations of Elvis's life.

The King of Rock 'n' Roll:

THE COMPLETE 50'S MASTERS

When BMG purchased RCA, they formed an international committee of record executives to clean up the Presley catalogue. Interested in presenting Elvis Presley's music as a chronicle of a culturally significant performer, the committee embarked on a multiproject goal that involved reissuing the music as close to its original form as possible.

Released in 1992, *The King of Rock 'n' Roll: The Complete 50's Masters* represents BMG's first significant restoration effort. Producers Ernst Mikael Jorgensen and Roger Semon searched the RCA vaults from Nashville to Indianapolis to Hollywood to find what they needed for this retrospective of Elvis Presley's complete 1950s output. The purity of the sound is a result of what the producers did not do to the master tapes as opposed to what they did do. The five-disc, 140-track compilation features all of Elvis's released recordings from that era as well as some alternate takes and rare live performances. A bound booklet by Presley biographer and music historian Peter Guralnik discusses the original recording sessions in depth.

Issued by the U.S. Postal Service on January 8, 1993, **the Elvis stamp** quickly became a popular and inexpensive piece of memorabilia. The stamp ballot, which featured illustrations of the two final stamp designs, has also become a desired collectible. The post office also offered a sheet of 40 stamps in a sleeve that looked like an album cover. Fans soon developed their own schemes for unique stamp collectibles, including writing erroneous addresses on Presley-stamped envelopes so they would be marked "Return to Sender."

The woman responsible for kicking off the Elvis stamp campaign was Pat Geiger. She began in 1983 with a letter to the U.S. Postal Service. Before she was through, more than 60,000 letters were written by stamp supporters. She wrote to celebrities seeking their support, but only Ann-Margret and her husband, Roger Smith, responded. Geiger endured endless interviews, often by an unsympathetic press, before her goal was met. Pat Geiger died in 2005. Fans everywhere owe her a debt of gratitude for her tireless efforts.